DES LAVELLE of Valentia, County Kerry, is a man of marine passions, and the beautiful Skellig Islands are listed ahead of the rest. A seaman, photographer, diving instructor and author, he – with his venerable boat, the *Béal Bocht* – has guided many thousands of visitors throughout the seas and islands of South Kerry. Absorbed by the wonders of wildlife, archae-ology and history that occupy every nook, cranny and salt wave of his surroundings, he has taken these topics on lecture circuits that stretch from the National Schools of his native Iveragh Peninsula to mainland Europe to the Irish American Cultural Institute Centres of some thirty American cities. His photographs and text also form the core of the Skellig Experi-ence Visitor Centre on Valentia.

Des retired from commercial boating in 2015. He, and his partner, Irene, live in Glanleam, Valentia Island. His North-facing windows offer a pan-orama of Valentia Harbour, Cromwell Point lighthouse, Dingle Bay and the Blasket Islands, but he is still drawn - on special summer days - to his Skellig Lorelei to the South-West.

Island Boy

DES LAVELLE
Island Boy

VALENTIA, SKELLIG AND

MY LIFE AT THE OCEAN'S EDGE

THE O'BRIEN PRESS
DUBLIN

First published 2022 by The O'Brien Press Ltd,
12 Terenure Road East, Rathgar, Dublin 6, D06 HD27, Ireland.
Tel: +353 1 4923333; Fax: +353 1 4922777
E-mail: books@obrien.ie
Website: obrien.ie
The O'Brien Press is a member of Publishing Ireland.

ISBN: 978-1-78849-286-7

7 6 5 4 3 2 1
26 25 24 23 22

Printed and bound in Poland by Białostockie Zakłady Graficzne S.A.
The paper in this book is produced using pulp from managed forests.

Published in:

DUBLIN
UNESCO
City of Literature

To four wonderful women.

CONTENTS

Letter-writing on my *Béal Bocht*.

PREFACE

Long before a portable typewriter, desktop computer, laptop or smartphone came my way, pen, paper, ink and pencil were never far from hand – on land or at sea – to record items of news, gossip, or equivalent world-shattering local data for my daughters, Céline and Linda, ever since they emigrated to the USA in 1984 and 1989 respectively. Both girls, irrespective of moving house numerous times, retained every letter of mine – even every scribbled, salt-water-blotched onboard note from many a boat trip! They were happy to share them with me again; and such are today's sources for many long-forgotten topics.

The laptop eventually came my way and accompanied me on my many US wanderings; long commentaries written from San Francisco or Butte, Montana, to friends in Ireland and England are also part of my data source.

As regards my childhood memories, they are just that: memories ... and there are not many contemporaries around to confirm or question them. Memories of old family topics feature too in today's thoughts, but some long-standing items of family folklore have even been omitted as – on inspection – their foundations were vague or even incorrect.

How long then has the writing of this memoir taken? Many rewrites and subsequent drafts passed some two years of the Covid Lockdown Era of 2020 and 2021. However, even as far back as 2005, much sorting of data and some related – if aimless – writing had been in progress.

Old photo albums proved helpful, rekindling memories of half-forgotten events; but the pity is that my early photos were mostly careless 'snaps'

– poor focus, much camera shake, and with little regard for composition or lighting. Poor storage of prints or colour slides was another failing; such considerations came only later. And, indeed, the cumbersome postal-processing options of earlier times did not facilitate any works of art despite my eventual evolution to Pentax and Nikon cameras in the now-antiquated film and colour-slide era. A flirtation with a Fuji Finepix digital camera was short-lived; I was just too focused on marine affairs to concentrate on the scenic magic or the contemporary topics that surrounded me.

My current photography device is an iPhone, one of a generation of iPhones that came into my life when a sailing capsize in our Wayfarer dinghy, *Steal Away*, in September 2010, left my earlier phone/camera somewhere in the middle of Valentia harbour, within sight of and within swimming distance of home.

Irene Rogers, my crew, was in the water too and laughed heartily at my decision to swim ashore rather than 'stay with the ship', my reasoning being that we both could survive the short swim, but I – ancient mariner of Valentia lifeboat days – could never survive the embarrassment of being rescued by Valentia lifeboat in the middle of Valentia harbour! So, waterproof portable VHF set notwithstanding, we inflated our life-jackets and swam for it. An obliging yachtsman came to our aid by towing the abandoned *Steal Away* to the safety of nearby Glanleam beach.

Today, a notebook or a scrap of paper is never far away because, as of old, if I don't jot something down as it occurs to me, it may be forgotten forthwith. And much has been forgotten already.

What is 'jotted down' here is but the bones of a Valentia lifetime.

Des Lavelle 2021

1

SURROUNDINGS

Astroll on the waterfront and village streets of Knightstown, Valentia Island, is the trigger for memories of days long ago when everything began for me.

It was a peculiar, contradictory beginning, where the surrounding adults of my childhood years were living out the final days of a colonial-type existence in the revered ambience of the Western Union Trans-Atlantic Cable Station, with many facilities at their disposal, while much of rural Kerry languished in relative, centuries-old immobility. Tennis tournaments and soirées on the lawn were the norm, together with a well-used billiard room, and a private library with subscriptions to a dozen international magazines, such as *Life* and *Illustrated London News*. Parties and dances aplenty were there for the Cable Station elders – in both the station property and on board grand visiting cable ships such as the *Lord Kelvin*, the *Marie Louise Mackay* and the *Edouard Suenson*.

Meanwhile, we – children of a new generation – were simply learning to be islanders. Playgrounds, gardens, tennis courts and sports fields were at our disposal too, but the nearby beach, literally across the road from home, was our real entertainment and our education – a life-template for this islander, who, in spite of opportunities, and often in the face of conventional wisdom, would remain an islander throughout the many social changes and lean economic periods witnessed in the environs of that Western Union Trans-Atlantic Telegraph Cable Station on Valentia Island in County Kerry.

My stroll inevitably lingers by those four terraces of twenty-three houses that – until closure in 1966 – were the Cable Station offices and staff dwellings for almost a century, and were my home for some sixty years – from 1934 to 1996.

Now, with but a few valued exceptions, many of these stately buildings languish in the alternative duty of seasonal holiday homes, and their many windows – once the eyes of a vibrant community – stare blindly at me, at the nearby waterfront and at the Kerry mainland across the harbour.

There were darker times, too. Following the closure of the Cable Station in February 1966, the entire property – offices and dwellings – went through a long phase of stagnation while it changed hands en bloc. It took some years before individual house purchases were possible, and rather longer before a far-sighted Waterford-based industrialist saw fit to buy the cable office

Overlooking the waterfront at Valentia Island, buildings formerly occupied by the Western Union Trans-Atlantic Telegraph Cable Station. Many now serve as holiday homes.

The spire of Knightstown's Church of the Immaculate Conception has provided practical transit guidance to local fishermen for many years.

building in 1975 and turn its main operations room into a mini-industry for the production of specialist adhesive tapes. Thus, Valentia Industries Ltd has provided employment for some six staff to this day.

But I linger not. In 'today mode', I continue homewards on a mile-long, well-travelled route along the waterfront and streets of Knightstown – a village that is the centre of my island, even if it is at the perimeter.

Familiar landmarks dot my way: the Church of the Immaculate Conception commands a goodly position on the shoreline promenade. Its Catholic ethos provides spiritual guidance for many of the island's 660 souls, and – preceding modern navigation aids by many generations – its conspicuous spire has provided practical guidance as a transit mark for local fishermen in their seasonal search for the harbour's once-rich scallop beds.

I received my initial, practical guidance in this church too in my baptism when I was christened with the names Desmond Gregory – even though there was never a Desmond or a Gregory in any line that I can trace. My First Communion also took place here, preceded by a well-rehearsed First Confession – a proficient guilt factory for innocents, suggesting that Heaven was a rather elusive quest, but that Hell came very readily indeed!

First Communion Day

Sunshine. Bunting in the breeze,
And tiny souls in white and bright in blue,
All fluttering, flitting to and fro,
On the best of First Communion Days,
And sad was I,
And silently passed by.
Mums and dads in smiles and Sunday-best,
Grandparents, wondering how years had passed.
And sad was I – not for my December years,
But for these angels' May-time fears:
Their First Confessions – told in trembling tones –
'Sinventions'! Yet intentions to atone!
Tentative stepping-stones
On a guilt-bound way!
'Perhaps, my child, you sometimes say
Bad words – or sometimes disobey?
And for forgiveness you must pray…'
And sad was I to see this bright array of souls
Inevitably dreading Hellfire's ghouls.
Unfounded fears! No God would ever so insist.
Nor stoop to such vindictiveness
As can a savant of the Roman Rules.

And sad was I,

And silently passed by.

I prayed, and asked the only God I knew,

To touch with wisdom those who shared the day,

That they might see it too…

Interpretations are not always true.

And sad was I,

And silently passed by.

With much pomp and ceremony, my Confirmation took place in this church too. And it included 'The Pledge' – a promise to abstain from all alcoholic drink. Was it a voluntary pledge? Was it 'for life' or was it time-limited 'until the age of twenty-five years'? I failed anyhow because a television advert for a 'Cool, Continental Lager' eventually won me away from the very straight and the exceedingly narrow.

For some two hundred years, the village's piers have withstood everything that wind and weather could throw at them.

As I round 'The Church Corner', the village's old harbour piers stand out robustly. They have withstood everything that wind and weather could throw at them for some two hundred years and have seen much commercial activity in the now-distant past.

In the pre-Second World War era, British trawlers docked here. Spanish trawlers, five and six abreast, sought shelter here in post-war years as the international fishing onslaught began in earnest in Irish waters. Here too, once upon a time, berthed local fishing boats – 13-man Seine netters, 7-man Followers, 4-man long-line fishers, 50ft ring netters, 65ft trawlers… The 1930s and 1940s saw coal ships here, delivering to storage depots and to individual homes, and saw us urchins following each cart to its destination so that we could then get a ride to the pier on the return trip to repeat the treat – and in the process, complete the day more grimy than the coalmen themselves. Here came the *MV Galtee* in 1958 with a cargo of ESB poles for the rural electrification of the island. Here berthed earlier cargo ships to export the island's world-famous Valentia slate during the halcyon days of quarrying in the mid-1800s, and incidentally to unload their ballast of flint and chert – typical stone products of the south of England – that would be used to trunk the Knightstown, Coombe, and Glanleam roads. Indeed, out-living various layers of failed, modern tarmac, fine examples of those totally alien pebbles in cream, tan, and black can still be seen here by anyone with a mindset odd enough to spend time contemplating the depths of a Valentia Island pothole!

I contemplate today's overall harbour scene, and question again the comparative inadequate shelter offered by the modern pontoon-built marina, spawned on some distant, cosseted drawing board far from the real-life experiences of Knightstown waters – the south-easterly gales that howl in from Ardcost or the nor'westers that rage through from Dingle Bay.

I pass the winter-silent car-ferry dock of 1996 origin, where an 18-vehicle

A south-easterly gale howling in Knightstown waters.

ferry facilitates islanders and visitors in their daytime summer travels, and cuts nearly 20km off the Valentia Bridge route to anywhere distant. What a far cry it is from memories of Cullotys' seasonal sales van from Cahersiveen – laden with winterwear or summerwear on a twice-yearly marketing foray to Valentia – being manhandled into a precarious nautical setting atop two planks laid across the gunwales of *The Thomas*!

Cullotys' van aboard *The Thomas* at Knightstown.

An architecturally pleasing public toilet is generally difficult to find. Worse than that, no public toilet of any design was in evidence in Knightstown until 2002. Now, the Knightstown waterfront boasts a custom-built one that blends perfectly in appearance, materials and design with the waterfront's related, ancient structures.

Nearby, 'The Hut', equally quaint in its centuries-old design, now enjoys a new and precious role as an exhibition window into the history and the equipment of Valentia's Coastal Cliff-rescue Services. Not always in this format, 'The Hut' was originally a shelter and a waiting room for the pedestrian or cycling ferry passengers of old. And much sheltering and many hours of waiting were endured there at the whim of weather and ferryman.

The nearby 'town clock', Victorian centrepiece of the waterfront, catches the eye. Since its restoration of recent times, I can believe the information it provides – the time and the hourly bell. But for generations, its four battered, rusty, silent, pockmarked faces told Knightstown that time had stood

Below left: Originally a shelter and a waiting room for ferry passengers, 'The Hut' has been converted into an exhibition window.
Below right: Today, the eye-catching Victorian 'town clock' marks the time with an hourly bell.

still since 1.53pm on an armed vandals' day-out in August 1922.

I stop at the nearby lifeboat station, admiring the magnificent Severn Class lifeboat, the *John & Margaret Doig*, resting at her moorings, and I recall times and voyages and sea conditions we endured as lifeboat crew volunteers in the 1950s, 1960s and 1970s in lifeboats of cumbersome – if robust – design that were slow, unmanageable vessels compared to the relative speedboats that constitute today's fleet. Recalling this station's 'half-mast' flag following the French lifeboat disaster on the coast of Les Sables-d'Olonne on 7 June 2019, I acknowledge again that all rescuers do not make it home.

The RNLI flag flies at half-mast in honour of those lost at sea.

The Royal Hotel has stood at 'The Hotel Corner' in Knightstown since the mid-nineteenth century.

At 'The Hotel Corner', I pass the principal Knightstown landmark, 'The Royal', where – depending on the century of your mindset – you can note that 'a comfortable hotel has been erected and is about to be fitted with baths' (1839), or 'you can find a comfortable inn, where you can eat and sleep in cleanliness' (1845), or you can learn that the hotel 'has been patronised by His Late Majesty King George and by their Royal Highnesses, the Prince and Princess of Wales and the Duke and Duchess of Connaught'; today, you will find that the services of dining room and accommodations of The Royal Valentia are second to none.

Knightstown's Market Street leads me uphill from the shoreline through a village remarkable for having been a planned development in the 1820s – an era when there was no such procedure as 'planning'. In the 1940s, Market Street could boast of five shops – Reidy's, O'Driscoll's, Miss Murphy's and two O'Sullivan's – that served the community well for foodstuffs, bakery products, butchery and minor hardware. But 'McCann's Boxes' cannot be forgotten either! This was a service from McCann's speciality store in Tralee whereby a commercial traveller – the names Norman McCann and Bertie

Hyland come to mind – came regularly to take orders for what might be called 'luxury goods'.

These orders – in individual tea chests or half-tea-chests – would follow by train to Renard Point, by ferry to Valentia, and be delivered to each Cable Station door by Ned Murphy and his horse cart.

I always noted well the day that 'McCann's Boxes' were due, because – even in those war years – there was always the hope of some additional treat. Invariably, of course, the goods in the neighbours' boxes – Mackeys', particularly – were more interesting than ours. Even sweet biscuits in the shape of letters! What fun to create my friends' names – and then eat them, one by one!

But McCann's service was too wonderful to last; it served my childhood years well, but faded in the 1950s.

Today, there is but one shop in Knightstown: Walsh's Foodstore is convenient for summer visitors, but vital to year-round citizens who otherwise would have to venture five miles or fifteen for their winter shopping.

Nearby, a post box at the corner of Reenellen replaces the long-gone Knightstown Post Office services, and a once-busy phone box at the same junction has long since been swept away – digitally and physically – by the avalanche of today's communications-media options. This particular phone box had been subject to some splendid malfunctions: for a period in 1990, a lucky caller could have free phone calls – and sometimes collect a modicum of extra change as well!

At this junction now, I can admire a memorial to one Maude Jane Delap (1866–1953), a precious Valentia lady of several generations ago who was exceptional in her time, being a renowned marine biologist in an age before marine biology was valued or even understood. Her family home, now in a derelict state, still stands at the end of this Reenellen lane.

Here too stands the ceremonial Village Pump in its splendid setting of a

Valentia-slate mini-plaza. But it never pumped a drop of water – not here anyhow; it is a latter-day, decorative creation of the 'Tidy Towns' effort.

I peer not into the nearby 'Slate Yard'. Once the centre of Valentia's vibrant and world-renowned slate export industry of the mid-1800s, the Slate Yard – over many years – has degenerated into a veritable junkyard of scrapped cars, abandoned boats, and related rubbish belonging to nobody, the responsibility of nobody, and quite beyond anybody's gentrification aspirations. No, I peer not and tread not in there today! A clean-up day must surely be somewhere on the horizon.

But, Slate Yard aside, I reflect on the tidiness and cleanliness of every street, road and edifice, and I say a silent 'Thank You' to Mayo-man Michael Egan, who has made Valentia his home since 1962, made Knightstown's tidiness and presentation his passion, and – with fundraising, hard work and even personal headaches – has taken the shabby and dejected village of 1983 and transformed it into an award-winner on the Tidy Towns stage.

Any such award monies were immediately re-invested in further gentrification; one such win in 1990 saw the purchase of a consignment of yellow paint, and I was given the job of painting all the bollards on the pier. It was almost an 'if it stands still, paint it' instruction, and I complied; not a careless driver has thumped a bollard ever since!

Tidy Towns

Discarded wrapper on the roadside grass,
Your colours click the link of hue and taste.
Your duty's done, but now the dreadful waste
Assaults the eyes of passers-by that pass.
Incredible how every lad and lass
Goes rushing by in real or pseudo haste,
Concerned not for what they have debased.

The roadside is a local looking-glass.
And who shall come collecting the debris
Of one-time joy and carelessness profound?
Why sometimes should the duty fall to me
To gather others' cast-offs from the ground?
If all are blind as those who will not see,
The roadside trash is beauty's burial mound.

Perhaps the enthusiasm for Tidy Towns was a little too keen at times. In the clean-up after a certain All-Ireland regatta in late 1990, an ancient wooden lobster crate that had lain – unused and unusable – around the Knightstown dock for quite some time, was mis-identified as festival trash and disposed of. However, when a peeved owner showed up, the Knightstown Tidy Towns Management – an organisation that never caught as much as a crab – had to invest in a new lobster crate.

At the junction of Market Street and Peter Street, I note two significant period terraces – the original coastguards' accommodations of generations ago, and their more modern equivalent, created as dwellings for the staff of the Valentia Coastguard Radio Station that has served seafarers well in marine communications and rescue since 1912.

In Jane Street, stands a large, old building – now embellished as a private dwelling. In a previous life, in the 1960s, it served a cinema; during World War II, it was an army billet; but originally it was 'The Fishermen's Hall', built in 1892 as a social centre and home-from-home for the many migratory fishing crews that followed the seasonal shoals of herring and mackerel from coast to coast – from the Isle of Man to Dingle Bay, and beyond.

In Peter Street stands another hall – its outline unchanged even in its new role as a modern dwelling; this is St Derarca's Parish Hall of 1906, once the busy social centre for all strands of Valentia society. Here, as teenagers, we waltzed our hearts out in dim gaslight to the button-accordion music of Paty-John, Padgen Murphy and Jimeen Murphy and to the violin of Jackie Sullivan; here, in our twenties – and in folded-down, thigh-length wellies upon returning at a timely hour from some seafaring mission – we danced 'Valentia set' upon 'Valentia set', and might afford ourselves but a breathless moment to slip down Peter Street to Mrs Greene for her vital buns-and-lemonade refresher options; here, in later years, played the next generation of button-accordion supremos, Nealie Donovan, Dan McCrohan and John Lyne; here, on piano accordion, played one Des Lavelle – aided by a homemade amplifier powered by a borrowed car battery; here – to 'imported' mainland musicians – we quick-stepped in the company of divers from all over Ireland and from as far away as Merseyside, Yorkshire, Devon and Cornwall when the Spearfishing Championship was in vogue; here, in the distant past, we enjoyed the products of visiting troubadours – the 'play crowds', as they were known – Coll and Dennehy, Paddy Dooley, Victor Acres. Here, on occasion, the Valentia Dramatic Society might stage a local presentation. Today, memories of the Hall's long-locked doors and cobwebbed windows are an eloquent confirmation that Island social life – as rural life everywhere – changed irrevocably a long time ago.

Further uphill, 'Boston's' pub completes the commercial offerings of Market Street, but the road junction here hides another Knightstown service – the atelier of Alan Ryan Hall, sculptor in stone and bronze, whose works are known worldwide.

Finally, crowning the village's architecture, the ageing Protestant Church of St John the Baptist, built in 1866, is witness to the fact that this tiny island outpost experienced immigration – if not ecumenism – in distant days.

Moving on uphill on the School Road out of the village, I pass the old Knightstown National School, built by my maternal great great grandfather, Patrick O'Sullivan, in 1861. Here, in the 1940s, I had much fun but minimal

The Church of Ireland Church of St John the Baptist was built in 1866.

education – the fun being entirely of boys' own making and inventiveness, the paucity of education being through no great inadequacy on the part of the educators. In earlier generations, the school attendance filled four classrooms; in my childhood years there, we occupied but three. Today, a new school in the island's central village – Chapeltown – is Valentia's source of primary education, while Knightstown's former school building, having benefited from fundraising and voluntary help, enjoys a new life as 'The Valentia Island Heritage Centre'.

There is one further striking historical terrace on my way – the 'Lighthouse Dwellings' of 1906. These were the homes of the families of the lightkeepers who manned the Inishtearaght and Skellig lighthouses until the progress of the 1970s and the automation of the 1980s took their inevitable toll and lighthouse keepers were no more. In that long terrace of eight fine houses, the windows are dark and dead on this winter's evening.

This striking terrace of houses was home to the families of the lightkeepers who, in their time, manned the Inishtearaght and Skellig lighthouses.

Perhaps I should have some sentimental feeling for this terrace, which may have been home to me as an infant for a short period. I say 'may' because none of the principal players in my life ever mentioned this era, or the family separation that ensued – not then, not since, not ever! Thus, the question of who was to blame for some fourteen lost years of 'normal' family life can never be answered.

Related generalisations are relatively easy to establish, though. In May 1931, Jim Lavelle, on being appointed as Assistant Keeper at Inishtearaght lighthouse, came to Valentia and was allocated a house in this eight-house terrace. Jim Lavelle and Eileen Renwick eloped and married in Killarney in 1933, and they were occupiers of – probably resident in – a house in 'The Dwellings' in 1934, when I was born. Thereafter, still Valentia-based, Jim served on Skelligs from August 1935 until March 1937. But upon Jim's subsequent transfer to the Old Head of Kinsale, Eileen did not accompany him; she remained in Valentia with her parents, Herbert and Annie Renwick, while Jim went on alone to serve later at Rockabill from December 1938, the Bailey from November 1942, Fastnet from October 1944, and Tuskar from February 1947.

At about fifteen years of age, and in the company of Eileen, I travelled to Rosslare and first met Jim Lavelle for a day or two during that Tuskar posting. I have only two memories from that brief visit – my surprise and relief upon discovering that he was a kind gentleman rather than the ogre I might have imagined, and my pleasure at being taught how to make a secure parcel, how to short-splice a three-strand rope, and how to set a good fire in an open grate.

Jim's subsequent posting as Principal Keeper on Aranmore Island (Donegal) from July 1951 finally saw a reunion with Eileen prosper. Likewise, a relatively 'normal' married life ensued thereafter while they were stationed at Mutton Island (Galway) from April 1953, Hook Head from June 1954, Tuskar from February 1957, Poer Head, County Cork, from 1965, and – in retirement – at Tarbert, County Kerry, from November 1967.

For my part, being Valentia based throughout the 1950s, I visited Jim and Eileen but infrequently. During their Aranmore posting, I visited them only once. My main recollections of that visit are of some futile wild-goose hunting with an heirloom Lavelle shotgun, and of buying a necklace in Letterkenny to take home as a gift to my girlfriend, Pat O'Neill of Cahersiveen. That the Donegal necklace fell to pieces after one outing was no bad omen; relationships prospered. My brother, Peter, was born in 1954 during Jim and Eileen's subsequent Hook Head sojourn. And Pat and I married in September 1956.

My stroll finally brings me to a welcome downhill section – the Glanleam

Road – where once dwelled the Knights of Kerry. Here, since the tenure of Robert Fitzgerald, the 17th Knight (1716–1781), they tirelessly promoted Valentia Island as the location for such unlikely bedfellows as the Trans-Atlantic Telegraph Cable Station, the lighthouse service base, the slate-quarrying industry, the Great Southern and Western Railway terminus at Renard Point, the island's first stone-built school, the harbour structures, the Valentia meteorological station, the marine radio station, the coastguard, the lifeboat service, and the occasional, appropriate hospitality for royal visits such as that of the Prince of Wales in 1858, and Prince Albert in 1869.

At last, I am nearly home, heading downhill into a cul-de-sac hideaway, where woodland and shrubbery and cliff and sandy beach lead to the sheltered shallows of Valentia harbour, and thence to Dingle Bay and the wild, wide Atlantic – and beyond, to the United States of America, where my daughters Céline and Linda have made their own happy homes since initial visits there in November 1984 and December 1989 respectively.

Happily, unlike the Irish emigration stories of previous generations, the now-frequent transatlantic crossings – by senior, junior and minor Lavelles (Maloneys) – no longer call for any 'American wakes'. Indeed, long before computer, laptop, iPad, smartphone, Viber and WhatsApp arrived upon the scene, pen, paper and postage stamps kept up a steady volume of correspondence, news, gossip – and sometimes *ráiméis* – that would maintain, enhance and invigorate bonds east and west across that Atlantic Ocean.

And in a further positive twist, my retirement location in Glanleam adds that ocean and the distant continent to my front garden, and affords me the time, inclination and opportunity to view far-off hills from both sides of the Atlantic – sometimes with rose-tinted spectacles, sometimes with a grain of salt.

2

GENES AND GENERATIONS

A treasured artefact in our family archives is a tattered handwritten note:

> Dear Mr. & Mrs. Renwick,
> By the time you get this, Eileen and I will be married.
> Hope you won't take things too bad.
> J. Lavelle.

A note from my father, Jim Lavelle, to my maternal grandparents.

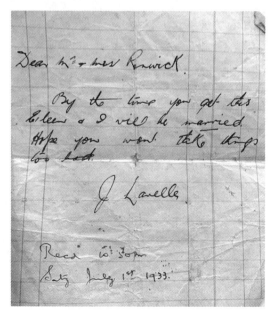

The document is undated, but a terse footnote in the spidery handwriting of my maternal grandfather, Herbert Renwick, pinpoints the time and the minute: 'Recd. 10.50 pm Saty. July 1ˢᵗ 1933.'

Eileen Renwick, born in 1916, was barely seventeen; Jim Lavelle was twenty-seven. And on 17 January 1934, I joined the party.

It was to be a peculiar party. By the time I could remember anything, my grandparents' then home – No. 18 Cable Terrace, Valentia Island – was 'home' to me. My grandfather, Herbert Renwick, was 'Dad', my grand-mother, Annie Renwick, was 'Mom', Eileen was my 'sister', and I didn't even know that a lighthouse keeper named Jim Lavelle existed – much less, a Lavelle grandmother in Dublin and a host of Lavelle aunts, uncles and cousins, some no farther away than County Limerick.

Surnames mattered not in my childhood. Yes, I was Des Lavelle, but the terms of endearment – 'Dad', 'Mom', 'Sister' – are still valid in my head some eight decades later – even if the real facts of life ultimately made their way into the realities of life a long, long time ago.

In 1934, the word 'dys-functional' did not appear in *The Oxford Dictionary of Current English, Third Edition.*

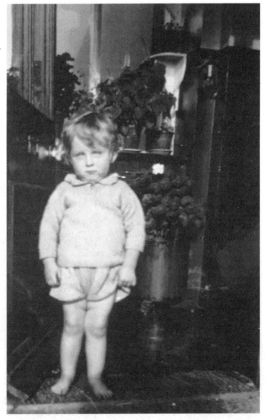

Me aged three, at home at no. 18 Cable Terrace, Valentia.

Nor was it needed. Dad was as good a dad as any small boy could want: he could fix things; he could make things. He made me many boats – out of timber off-cuts, out of driftwood, out of cork, out of recycled paint cans. He made masts and sails for them. He made oars for them. He could solder up model anchors and propellers with the heat of a roaring, paraffin-fuelled blowlamp and a great soldering iron – itself homemade from a lump of recycled copper. He could fix broken woodwork of any kind with a hot concoction of smelly glue, allegedly made of cows' hooves. He could read me endless bedtime tales from my favourite books, until – mercifully – I would fall asleep without the horror of being alone in the dark. He could win me from tears to laughter by pretending to chase a bee around the garden when I split and disfigured two right-hand fingertips by getting them stuck in

Mom's monstrous clothes wringer during a Monday morning's laundry routine. He could keep me entertained for hours in his under-the-stairs photographic darkroom as he developed new negatives and made contact prints of old antiques of the 1930s – including images of Italian Air Marshal Balbo's reconnaissance seaplanes moored in Valentia harbour.

I learned much from Dad, but one skill I could never match was the meticulous way he draped his

In the 1940s, with some of the many boats Dad made for me.

31

daywear on a bedside chair when he retired at night. It seemed to me that his various garments just lay there as tidily as if he had evaporated out of them, and all would be instantly ready in the morning so that he could re-constitute himself into them again without any of the normal labours of pulling on his vest, shirt, long johns, pants, cardigan – and his jacket with the leather patches on the elbows. He was once a London fireman, he told me; perhaps that explained it. But that was long before he became a 'telegrapher' in the Western Union Trans-Atlantic Cable Station on Valentia Island, County Kerry.

Without doubt, Mom was the boss. She had, after all, managed to convert Herbert to Catholicism, and she ran a fairly tight ship in matters of church attendance for mass and other religious duties. Her world was entirely within the home, with no public function other than her voluntary church duty of 'doing the altar' in the month of November. My Friday duty during that month was to call at Mrs Dan Walsh's house in Jane Street on my way home from school, to collect the great bunch of golden chrysanthemums that – lovingly arranged by Mom's able hands – would decorate the altar of the Knightstown Catholic church for the following week. Today, wherever in the world I encounter the scent of a chrysanthemum, I see a flash of Mrs Walsh's garden and a vision of a small boy, inundated in a great bunch of golden flowers, dawdling homeward through the fields like some modern cartoon version of Interflora.

The shamrock of St Patrick's Day was a further excess of plant life that stands out from the same era. Dad was the champion finder of wild shamrock, and Mom was inevitably the wearer of the world's greatest spray of it. Her diminutive frame was scarcely visible behind the swathe of green adorning her lapel as she trudged off to mass on St Patrick's Day, with me in tow. I was obliged to wear it too, albeit in more modest proportion. But an embarrassingly large St Patrick's Day Badge – a green cardboard harp with golden tassels – made up the shortfall. It was an overall ensemble that left me with a lifelong distaste for the 'outward shows' of life – long before Shakespeare's similar sentiment was forced laboriously upon my memory in *The Merchant of Venice* of the 'Inter Cert' curriculum of 1949.

'Oh, Moses!' was the nearest thing to an expletive that Mom ever uttered, but that was enough to get everyone's attention – particularly mine. I seldom fell foul of her, at least not after one childhood Christmas occasion when – dressed in the full Sioux regalia with a turkey-feathered war bonnet, and armed with an appropriate bow, arrow and lance – I attacked her newly delivered, four-stone bag of flour and left it bleeding to death on the kitchen floor. 'Ambush and run' being the common tactic of my Wild West characters, I ran, and – in a total reversal of The Little Big Horn battlefield scene

– myself and an imaginary Sioux Nation had to take ignominious refuge under a bed when Mom charged like Custer's 7th Cavalry.

It was Eileen who took me to Mrs Coughlan's room at Knightstown National School on my first day. My dog, Rinty, a faithful terrier of no great pedigree, came along too, 'to keep me company'. But when Eileen had left and Mrs Coughlan had thrown

In full Sioux regalia, with a turkey-feathered war bonnet.

Rinty out of the classroom and shut the door, I suddenly realised that I was trapped – with no room to manoeuvre, no room to escape. It was a traumatic day that constituted one of my earliest life-lessons: 'Check the emergency exit' or 'Don't burn your boats!'

A year or two later, I would learn something equally useful in the same room and in the same Mrs Coughlan's tender care. She was calling the rolls and made some error in her entry.

'Has anyone got an eraser?' she asked. We were not supposed to have erasers

With my faithful terrier, Rinty, who accompanied me on my first day at school but was soon thrown out by Mrs Coughlan.

but, co-operative in the extreme, I put up my hand and offered mine. She took the eraser, thanked me, made her corrections – and then confiscated my precious possession. Such treachery – and *in loco parentis* too! This memorable event did nothing to improve Mrs Coughlan's standing in my six-year-old head, but it added another tweak to the spiral of my DNA: 'He who has been bitten by the crab will not offer his toe a second time.'

Notwithstanding the accent on prayer in those early days – the Hail Mary and the Our Father, at least – it was in this same room that my faith in said pursuit was tested … and failed.

To raise money for the African Missions – or 'The Black Babies', as was the common term – Mrs Coughlan announced a 'Grand Raffle for the Splendid Prize of a Model Aeroplane', handmade by 'Johno' Neill of the Valentia (Coastguard) Radio Station! It was a replica of a German reconnaissance plane that could be seen almost daily from the Station's location on Dohilla cliffs, as it traversed the local, offshore waters, searching for easy targets amongst incoming allied shipping, and credited with the sinking of the 2,218 cargo ship, *Latymer,* four miles west of the Skelligs on 2 October 1940. It was an event noted and logged by the Inishtearaght lighthouse crew, Tony Walsh of Valentia among them – and by the men of the Coast Watching Lookout Post on Valentia's Bray Head.

02.10.1940. 15.20 hrs. Sighted vessel 14 miles NW of Post, showing distress signals, and seemed to be on fire. Guards and Fenit lifeboat notified.

Oblivious to these harsh facts of nearby warfare and destruction, I happily paid my penny, or my 'thrippenny bit', or my 'tanner' – or perhaps it was even as much as a 'bob' for a raffle ticket – and resorted to prayer. I prayed by day and by night that I might win the Great Prize that was on display daily on the classroom windowsill. I prayed. And I prayed.

But my prayers didn't work! Somebody else got Johno's lovely plane, with its beautiful black crosses on the underwing and its splendid landing wheels, made from the screw-on caps of two Brasso bottles.

My resilience was further tested and forged in the fire in those early days by the inevitable schoolyard disagreements and related comments that aired the family secrets of all and sundry. But even if I didn't understand the 'B' word very well, I was happy with the Mom and Dad that I had. Furthermore, most taunts could readily be silenced by airing the perpetrators' own laundry lists: 'You're half a proddy, proddy, protestant anyhow' was a particularly useful counterattack that seemed to be appropriately derogatory at that age and at that time.

Childhood was not about arguments or name-calling, though; it was all about boats – and the enjoyment they gave. Wooden boats were everywhere in Valentia Island pursuits of the 1940s – on the beaches, by the pier, on the water, on the moorings, and in the blood. There may have been only four cars on that early Valentia Island – owned by two doctors, a teacher and the parish priest – but there were ten times as many boats. These included ferry boats, cattle boats, sailing boats, rowing boats, fishing boats, seine boats, four-oar boats, and boats of no denomination at all.

Almost every able-bodied man among Dad's colleagues and contemporaries in the Cable Station had a boat – a punt of 14 feet or more – well used in summer to fill the substantial daytime leisure hours that fitted into the station's twenty-four-hour operation and its consequent, rotating, eight-hour shifts. And for every boat on its mooring on the Cable Station's waterfront, there was a flat-bottom dinghy on the beach. And these giddy vessels were the first step in our juvenile nautical education. We rowed them; we fell out of them; we capsized and salvaged them. And we survived. Only then did we graduate to the larger punts and the access to the local wide world that they offered – even occasional visits to that exciting, out-of-bounds Cathedral Cave on Doulus Head.

We seafaring 'Musketeers' of those days, who had been neighbours since we first could walk, were four in number: Colin Myles-Hook, Ronnie Longland, Adrian Mackey and myself. To complete the gang, add in a seasonal, visiting minor Musketeer, John Condon, who joined us regularly in summer at his grandmother's home, to share every exploit.

Colin was the envy of the other three because – to complement his model boats – he had such riches as a model railway for the days when rain confined him indoors.

Ronnie won the admiration and courtship of everyone because he alone had a football. He also was the only one to do his school homework, and generously provided all and sundry with the answers daily at 'The Parson's Gate' – our essential morning rendezvous before we slunk into class at Knightstown National School. In this, he bravely ran the risk that if he got something wrong, so did everyone, whereupon Ronnie would suffer double trouble at the teacher's hands for providing the 'data services'.

Adrian was admired for his Public Relations skills in meeting and greeting strangers – something that would invariably get him on stage in St Derarca's Hall for some one-line part whenever a travelling theatre company – or 'play crowd' – came to the island.

If I was envied for anything, it may have been for my books, because whatever the privations of wartime, Christmas always meant books for me: *The Golden Gift Book, Stories for Boys, The Wonder Book of Wonders...* I had books that told of vertical take-off flying machines in an age before today's helicopters were even fiction; books that spoke of space travel a generation or two before the first Russian 'Sputnik' crossed our night skies; books that took me to the frontiers of the world, the ocean, the islands, the skies, and the great American West – books, indeed, bearing the inscription 'Xmas 1938' and 'Xmas 1941', in Dad's hand, that would live on to entertain daughters Céline and Linda in their time, my now-adult grandsons, Sam and Jackson Maloney, in their time, and that still today occupy a niche in San Francisco and Butte, Montana, as treasured family artefacts.

My tin-can-made toy boat, negotiating the shallows of the local beach with the aid of a long bamboo and length of string, was generally the most successful local voyager, capable of ferrying a cargo of periwinkles safely from the 'End Gate' to the 'New Terrace' in many weathers, and this fact may also have gained me some points in the boyhood scale of boating skills.

Musketeer John, being the youngest of the bunch, was the envy of nobody; he just followed us around, got in our way, etching his plaintive call, 'Wait for meeeee...' into the vernacular of the fast-moving posse. He also – mistakenly – thought that we older boys had much to teach him.

Two girls, Eileen and Mary, were associates of our Musketeer group by virtue of location and age. But age was the bogey: they were not interested in boats; they were not interested in football; they were not interested in model railways; and if there might have been opportunities to learn anything useful from them, they were wasted on us – or on me anyhow.

In those years, any modicum of information-to-come was welcome

Eileen and Mary were associate Musketeers by virtue of location and age.

and exciting. The Salesman-with-the-Bike was a gentleman of apparent Asian origin who occasionally visited Valentia and did his selling from a suitcase on the back of a bicycle. But it was the nature of his wares that interested us boys so much: 'Nice ladies' panties, every size,' was his sales pitch as he accosted everyone he met on doorstep and roadside. Save our young souls – ladies' panties were unmentionables, and it was probably bordering on Mortal Sin just to see them being taken out of his case for display purposes! And Mom's eventual sex-education talk didn't really clarify any boys/girls knickers/underpants topics either: 'It's OK,' she said; 'It's OK to play with girls – so long as you respect them…' I didn't know what she was talking about – and I didn't dare ask. It seemed like this was something I should know already.

Equally vague – but somehow memorable in tender years – was a moment in a quiet corner in another girl's company. 'You know, Des,' she said, 'in a place like this, I could tempt you, or you could tempt me…' Tempt? The only temptations I knew in those days were the six-for-a-penny toffees in Tady Driscoll's shop – particularly during Lent. I didn't have any – and neither did she – so the strange conversation petered out.

Even at an age when I should finally have been getting smart, I remember sitting in Valentia cinema near yet another sweet girl who kept leading my hand towards her chest. I didn't know what on earth all that was about either! And nor did I ask. In the cinema's uncomfortable bench seats, this was much too difficult a gymnastic test, and besides, the weekly cinematic escapades of Wallace Beery and similar Wild West champions hunting down assorted bandits were more deserving of my undivided attention.

Indeed, even now, in my ninth decade, a degree of the same innocence lingers: I hear occasional expressions – again relating to latter-day human interactions – and I still don't know what they are talking about. Nor do I dare to ask.

3

BOATS AND WAR GAMES

As boys, when we weren't coursing the beach as apprentice sailors, we were marching the roads as apprentice soldiers, rubbing shoulders with the rank and file of the Irish Army garrison that was stationed and housed in vacant Cable Station properties on Valentia during the Second World War, as a protection for Valentia Island's centres of telegraph cable and radio communication.

Protection there was – after a fashion. On sleepless nights, come midnight or later, and hearing local Valentia revellers in full voice wandering home along the Shore Road in front of the Cable Station, a sentry's challenge would suddenly ring out: 'Halt! Who goes there?' The revellers did not halt; they didn't even break the tempo of their songs – except, perhaps, to include an occasional volley of pointed political or personal taunts. Even the metallic rattle of a .303 Enfield rifle bolt, suggesting that the sentry now had a live round in the chamber, could not silence these passing champions.

'A hostile incursion was repulsed' or 'The army's bluff was called'; it all depends on who tells the story. Anyhow, nobody ever got shot, and the revelry and rivalry continued on their merry, nocturnal way, until the revellers faded into the distance, only to surface again on the following night or – in more robust form – at the next local social function.

Neutrality, security or such political considerations did not interest me much in 1939–46. I romped around with my Musketeer companions in situations that could never happen today – a bunch of children, totally unrelated to any of the army personnel, running unattended around the barracks. Into the guardroom we would wander, where there were *real* bayonets and *live* ammunition at hand. Into the force's only truck we would jump to hitch a three-mile ride for the changing of the guard at the Coastguard 'Valentia Radio' Station on the island's northern cliffs. In to the army's medical

The Musketeers – myself, Colin and Adrian – with Dasher O'Connor.

orderly, Danny O'Meara, we would limp on occasion, to have knuckles and knees bandaged, as I was reminded many years later when the same Danny O'Meara – having spent his entire post-war life in Australia and New Zealand – made a holiday trip to Ireland in August 1999, and visited me to chat into the late hours about those old times.

In memory, I could smell again the disinfectant in the front, upstairs room over the Cable Station office that had been Danny's 'surgery'. Into the army kitchen I could again stroll with my Musketeer companions, where the chef – known only as 'Rashers' – kept giant cauldrons and kettles eternally bubbling. Into the wooden-built mess-hall, which then occupied most of the back garden of Cable Station house No. 13, I could slink again, savouring mealtimes there and enjoying again the great enamel mugs of tea and lashings of the shop bread with such butter and strawberry jam as the civilian ration books of the time could not provide. Into the military shower facility, we Musketeers would sneak – a corrugated-iron amendment to the garden shed of the same No. 13 – to risk being scalded or chilled to the bone by the peat-fuelled, hand-pumped contraption that offered boiling or freezing water, with rare intermediate choices. Into the army pantry we would daily make our way, where the endless, careless peeling of potatoes prompted even us boys to wonder who exactly got the most food per potato – the hungry soldier or Con Mack's pigs which were charged with the duty of disposing of the inch-thick peels.

The only activity that might keep us out from under the Army's and Danny O'Meara's feet in those days would be an offer of some real boating. Dad had a punt, and its annual seasonal launch was an eagerly awaited event. He also had an ancient outboard engine, a rather early model in the evolution of marine propulsion, and – notwithstanding its propensity to administer near-fatal electric shocks to anyone within reach – summer days saw him spending hours trying to force life into that obstinate machine. He

Cathedral Cave on Doulus Head was a popular boating destination for us.

was up against many odds: the plug could be wet, the coil damp, the carburettor flooded, the jets choked, the impeller blocked, the 'points' stuck or the shear-pin sheared. Indeed, in a wartime black market, the petrol itself could be something less than plentiful, and frequently much less than legitimate.

When the outboard worked, it was a thrill to ship our oars and cruise along at three miles an hour, heading to the nearby Beginish Island, which offered us two splendid, sandy beaches. If Valentia wasn't already heaven, Beginish was the ultimate: sheltered waters on one shore, Atlantic breakers on the other, dunes and sandhills to wander, terns' and gulls' nests to find, ruins of ancient buildings to discover as wind and weather eroded scanty vegetation, cliffs of basalt and old red sandstone to climb, old boats and bits of boats to examine, spent bullets to find in the sand near 'The Target'

Beginish Island, with its two sandy beaches, was heaven for boys in boats.

– a training range for forces of an earlier date. And everywhere, a splendid excess of 1940s sunburn was on offer – enough, in my case, to ensure a remunerative workload for dermatologists and plastic surgeons into the following millennium.

Casual visitors to Valentia or to our Cable Station enclave were few and far between in the 1940s. Someone's cousin – male or female – might visit from Dublin or elsewhere and create a momentary stir by beating us roundly at tennis or outswimming us on Beginish beach. They would soon be forgotten. But the visiting 'play crowds' of the era would be remembered forever! When these travelling actors brought their drama and variety to St Derarca's Parish Hall in Valentia, we Musketeers would occasionally qualify to attend one of their nightly offerings as a special treat – even if only in the one-shilling backless benches.

Ghosts of those 'fit-up' actors of the 1940s and 1950s still linger in Peter Street surroundings today. In the quiet of nightfall, I hear the bustle as the patrons pour into the hall, their half-crowns or their shillings swiftly accumulating in a well-battered biscuit tin under the beady eye of a troubadour. Still pungent is the smell of the paraffin-lamp stage-lighting; still reverberating is the off-tune, borrowed piano, thumping out the obligatory opening chorus or the crescendo of sound effects when some foul dramatic deed was done.

Typically, it was at these moments of enthusiasm that the rumpus would break out at the back of the hall – invariably along the army/local divide. Stools and chairs would be hurled aside as men rushed to join the fray, as women rushed to escape it, and as the Garda Síochána and the military police waded in to sort it all out. Splendid entertainment all this – especially for a ten-year-old boy. But the permanent 'Catch-22' was that we Musketeers, having stealthily sneaked forward underneath the 'two-bob' bench seats to secure a two-and-sixpenny chair and a better view of Adrian's performance – possibly as the dying child in the reliable old tear-jerker,

East Lynne – were then too distant to see the finer details of the real action down the back.

Apart from theatrical skills, though, the travelling 'play crowd' must – retrospectively, or posthumously, perhaps – be awarded a prize for inventiveness and for 'Keeping the Show on the Road', even when one or more of the cast might be 'unavoidably detained'. Who else could muster a 'Local Talent Competition' at the drop of a hat, giving the audience not only the duty of selecting the quarter and semi-finalists, but having us sit through it all again as the winner's rendition was played back on 'the latest wire recorder'? Who else could invent a 'Smoking Contest' to fill another blank hour? Imagine five or six local heroes lined up on the stage, each given a Woodbine and a match, with the offer of a Grand Prize of a carton of Sweet Afton for the first man to have the cigarette smoked down to the butt! Cheats who hadn't had a smoke – or the price of it – for a week would happily dawdle and enjoy the free Woodbine, but serious prize-hunters would drag that cigarette into furnace fury until it disappeared before our eyes, and a champion was proclaimed.

I was not interested. At some tender age, I had already learned the lesson that 'Smoking Can Seriously Damage Your Health'. In my case, not cigarettes, not tobacco, but dry peat in a pipe – homemade from a hollowed-out cork and a bamboo stem! I remember lighting my pipe, and I remember taking one great draught. My world spun around, nausea overtook me, and I passed out like a light. It was army peat, of course, which may have accounted for its potency. But the cure was total.

There were no easy cures for the worries of the ongoing, surrounding warfare – and it wasn't just matters of aircraft activity or surface shipping. From the Dohilla clifftop, many a German submarine was also sighted in Dingle Bay – not necessarily U-35 which landed twenty-eight crewmen from the

4,990-ton Greek-registered *Diamantis* in Ventry on 4 October 1939, nor U-38 which landed German agent Walter Simon some miles further east on 13 June 1940, nor the unidentified submarine that landed German agent Wilhelm Preetz near Minard on about 26 June 1940.

Liaison between German submarines in Dingle Bay and their airborne colleagues overflying the area – be it on matters of weather information or Allied shipping targets – brought the war very near to Valentia and exacerbated the very real fear that Ireland would soon be invaded, whether by the British who wanted use of the Irish ports to protect their western flanks or by the Germans seeking enhanced access to the transatlantic Allied convoys and a consequent pincer attack on Britain.

The worries of the surrounding adults of my life were not allayed by any reports from Bray Head Coast-watch Lookout Post:

15.10.1940. 12.30 hrs. Sighted twin-engine bomber, 5 miles West of Lookout Post, going south at 2,000ft. Markings: Swastika and black cross.

16.10.1940. 10.00 hrs. Sighted twin-engine bomber, one mile East of Lookout Post. Markings: Black cross under both wings.

It was this non-stop warfare activity that – two months later – caused the nearest thing to an invasion that the Valentia army garrison encountered. The story begins in the log of the Bray Head Lookout Post, detailing some peculiar ship movements quite at variance with the usual furtive, zigzag courses of Allied cargo vessels as they strove to avoid hostile submarines and aircraft:

03.12.1940.

13.55 hrs. Sighted large cargo boat 10 miles West of Post. Going

North.

16.30 hrs. Cargo boat reported at 13.55 is now stopped 10 miles NW of Post.

17.40 hrs. Cargo boat reported at 13.55 and 16.30, still stationary 10 miles W of Post.

18.20 hrs. Vessel 2 miles NE of Post, going NW.

18.50. Vessel reported at 18.20 altered course 2 miles NW of Post, going east in direction of Valentia harbour.

The army garrison's alarm bells began ringing in the early hours of 4 December 1940, when a boatload of seamen landed on the rocky shore of Valentia at Cúas na mBó – near the 'Cable Hut' where the sensitive transatlantic telegraph cables entered the sea, and equally near to the vital marine communications centre, Valentia (Coastguard) Radio Station. 'Code Red' it might be termed in modern language, sending army reinforcements rushing from Knightstown to cordon off the entire area, and preparing to repel an invasion – until the 'invaders' were identified as a war-weary civilian crew who had chosen to abandon their leaking Yugoslav-registered vessel, the 2,000-ton cargo ship *Cevriti* (alternative spellings are noted elsewhere), and its cargo of salt fish, in Dingle Bay, and take their chances on the rocky coast of Kerry.

A brief detention was their lot, and being civilian non-combatants, they would not even be destined for internment in the Curragh Camp. Consequently, they enjoyed considerable temporary hospitality in Valentia and Cahersiveen before sliding away into the murk of 'The Emergency'. For them, it was a far better fate than being torpedoed by German submarines, bombed or machine-gunned by German aircraft, drowned at sea in their ramshackle cargo ship – or shot on sight by the Irish Army at Cúas na mBó.

And their visit was not without local fringe benefits. Their abandoned lifeboat yielded treasure for local beachcombers, in the shape of tinned fruit, chocolate and even a compass, and their abandoned 56-year-old *Cevriti*, discovered still drifting and unmanned in Dingle Bay and brought to anchor in Valentia harbour by a boarding party from the Irish Navy's *Fort Rannock*, was a further economic benefit: local men were hired to unload her cargo of bagged salt fish so that temporary 'concrete box' repairs could be carried out on *Cevriti's* leaking hull. Watchmen were hired to guard the vessel by night to prevent looting – only to find themselves locked into a cabin while various goods disappeared anyhow. Eventually, the *Cevriti* was towed away for a major refit. Her passing was again noted by the Coast-watch Lookout:

> 8th January 1941. 13.00 hrs. Yugoslav boat that was in Valentia Harbour is in tow, going South, Irish flag at masthead, Yugoslav flag at stern.

The Irish flag would stay: the *Cevriti* was refitted in Dublin and became the *Irish Beech* of a fledgling Irish Shipping Ltd. But she brought her troubles with her: the temporary 'concrete box' repair carried out at Valentia would not be the only one; when she was finally scrapped in 1948, over 60 'concrete box' repairs were discovered in the hull.

Bursts of machine-gun fire near the radio station in the dark of a stormy night triggered another full military alert – manning the sentry posts, calling up reinforcements from the main camp, and sealing off the whole townland of Dohilla – until the recurring 'machine-gun fire' was identified as a steel barrel rolling over a corrugated iron roof in the gale.

Real machine-gun fire did burst forth from the sentry post on the roof of the Cable Station on one occasion when the gunner saw an 'enemy aircraft' homing in on the post. And the gunner's aim was true. But there was no loss of life, only some embarrassment – the 'enemy aircraft' he had brought down was a weather balloon. If this was November 1941, the overenthusiasm may have been related to another entry in the Coast-watching log:

11.11.1941. 11.15 hrs. Information received that 28 barrage balloons, broken adrift from Plymouth, likely to drift towards Eire.

Real evidence of war was everywhere in those years – particularly on our beaches. Ships' life-rafts with no occupants but with emergency stores of tinned chocolate and biscuits were washed in; bales of rubber were washed in; barrels of oil and petrol were washed in – all to the delight of the beach-combers who might find them. Survivors of the *Latymer* – sunk by that reconnaissance plane whose handmade replica had been the much-coveted prize in Mrs Coughlan's Grand Raffle – claimed that their cargo had included fifty-six hogsheads of brandy, but if these particular spoils of war ever came ashore, nobody local shouted from the rooftops about it. True, a consignment of spirits did come into the 'safe-keeping' of the Army at that time, and coincidentally, Ballymullen Barracks in Tralee was the scene of quite memorable overindulgence, with the morning parade being a sobering exercise indeed. In the words of one of the closest observers, Medical Orderly Danny O'Meara, 'It put a lot of blokes on their backs.'

The widespread loss of life, ships and aircraft in the immediate area told us that the war was never far away, but for me, the war was at home too: Dad, as a Londoner who had come to Valentia in the early 1900s to work in the Cable Station, had a particular interest, and had a wall-mounted map of Europe, highlighted with pin-up flags of the various engagements and 'fronts'. As a source of information, he also had a homemade 'wireless', filled with glowing valves, condensers, resistances and coils, all joined together by a thousand soldered joints, and powered by 'wet' and 'dry' batteries. It was as big as a domestic dishwasher – and emitted more groans and squeaks than any mechanical machine, but the BBC came through, as did the 'Germany Calling' propaganda broadcasts of 'Lord Haw-Haw'.

If Dad only knew then what we know now about 'spin doctors' and 'fake news', he might have taken both sources with a bit more salt – and adjusted his flagged battlelines accordingly.

The Army was a good source of supply for .22 bullets. Adrian's father, Freddy Mackey, had a rifle, but 'ammo' was scarce in those days, and the Army's range-practice logs of B Company, 15th Infantry Battalion, were often 'amended' to fill this civilian need. But if bullets were scarce, rabbits were plentiful; we often set out for Beginish Island with one bullet but came home with two rabbits. A more entertaining use of the rare bullet was to prize off the lead projectile, crimp the shell-case closed, and insert it into one of the occasional sods of turf that we were obliged to bring to school in winter. It was a kind of Russian Roulette because nobody knew when the 'charged' sod would find its way into the open hearth.

Our National School master, Johnny Mawe, is in Heaven today because he served his purgatory in those times when we reached fifth, sixth and seventh class. His habit was to stand with his back to the fire – and he had to stand close indeed to glean any thermal unit of heat from the smouldering sparks. Suddenly the smoking grate would erupt in a minor explosion, enveloping the master – and anyone nearby – in a cloud of yellow ashes. Thereafter, until he recovered his composure, he would shun the fire, and stand with his back to the front row of sixth class while he was teaching the fifth – providing a splendid opportunity for someone in that front row to pin a rabbit's tail to the back of his coat. Such dexterity! Such courage!

The school clock was another of our targets – literally. One strand of elastic, surreptitiously extricated from the already meagre waistband of a 1940s pair of underpants, made a splendid catapult for hurling small darts of folded paper at assorted targets, and with careful aim, the chime mechanism of the schoolroom clock – which had not sounded of its own volition since the 1860s – would suddenly ring out loud and clear above the master's head.

Master Mawe had once regarded me as a scholar who might have had potential, but his eventual frequent comment, 'Des, you're as bad as the rest of them now', clearly suggested that all was lost. Others came in for more scathing comment: 'You'll be a fool all your life' was his frequent assessment of another scholar, who went on in life to disprove the prediction roundly. 'Rotter' was his fiercest epithet; it was meted out with great regularity. And when that failed to induce scholarly productivity, Master Mawe had his substantial hazel rod for 'six-of-the-best' chastisement – until Paddy Reidy, long before he set out on life's road as a missionary priest in the Philippines, disposed of the hated cane in the boys' open-cesspit toilet.

History and Geography were the master's favourite subjects. They were not mine. In my mind, the master's pale heroes, such as Brian Ború of 1014 or Daniel O'Connell of 1840, were totally eclipsed by such legendary characters as Wyatt Earp and Doc Holliday of 1881, who filled my bedtime reading hours with such excitement. How dull I found it to try to memorise the fact that the island of Ireland measured some 300 miles in length by about 150 miles in width, when I knew that just across the nearby Atlantic Ocean – which began only fifty paces from my doorstep – the vast plains of America stretched onwards forever! This conflict of interest had only one conclusion: instead of studying my History and Geography of Ireland, I spent serious hours absorbing the intimate details of every Wild West story – fact or fiction – that I could beg, borrow or trade.

It interested me little that there had been copper mining on the coast of the nearby Beara peninsula of County Cork from prehistoric times, but what exciting stuff it was to read of the early copper-mining years in that rip-roaring town of Butte, Montana – the arson, the sabotage, the claim-jumping, the murder, and the riches beyond belief. My distraught teacher could not interest me in the fact that there was coal in Castlecomer, County Kilkenny. But at the drop of a hat, I could have quoted in hundreds of millions of dollars the fabulous output of the 1859 gold and silver strikes of the Comstock Lode at Virginia City, Nevada, and Gregory's Gulch, fifty miles west of Denver, Colorado.

Master Mawe's History lecture might begin: 'In 1836, The Poor Law Commission reported that out of Ireland's population of eight million people, nearly 2,500,000 were on the verge of starvation.' Then he would pause. 'What other big catastrophe beset the Irish population in the following years?' Nobody answered. Nobody ever answered unless picked upon. I knew that in 1836, some two hundred Texas revolutionaries – Davy Crockett and Jim Bowie among them – had fought their way into history, trying to hold out against Mexico's General Antonio Lopez de Santa Anna at the Battle of the Alamo; but I was not going to mention that.

'I'll make it easier for you; Des, what happened in Ireland in the years of 1845 and 1847?'

'There was a famine, sir?' I knew that much, but I could not elaborate.

'Yes, Des, there was a famine; and millions died of starvation and further millions were forced into emigration...'

But already I was not paying attention. 'Emigration' was a trigger-word, and I was thinking of what those famine emigrants did when they sailed into the ports of New York or Quebec or up the Delaware river to Philadelphia. Did they settle there? Did they soon hear the exciting news of James W. Marshall's 1848 discovery of gold at Captain Sutter's mill in California? Did they put to sea again and seek those Californian riches via Cape Horn or across the disease-deadly Isthmus of Panama? Did they join the mainland's westward Gold Rush through swamp, desert, plain, mountain and violence?

Lessons went on, daydreams went on. If Johnny Mawe and I had ever stopped to think about it, we would have realised that our tracks were not too far apart; his was the track of the National School curriculum of 1944 and mine was the track westward across the Atlantic and onwards to the Rocky Mountains – and the Pacific Ocean. It was all History and Geography – except that *Stories for Boys* was my initial textbook, and Zane Grey and Lorrie Lamour, classic novelists of the 'Wild West', were my real History and Geography teachers.

Thus, academia – Valentia-style – was not for me. But other valuable lessons, not on any curriculum, came free-gratis on our route to and from school, as our attention in the late 1940s focused on the foreign fishing fleet that then began to appear in Valentia harbour for shelter and services as its fishing activities expanded right up to – and within – the miniscule three-mile limit of the Irish coast.

British trawlers from Swansea, Milford Haven, Lowestoft, Grimsby and Hull were already such regular callers that various skippers, such as 'Russian John' and 'Jimmy Mac', were household names locally – and were always good for a hamper of splendid hake in barter for some local services. But in an area and during an era that boasted only a few small, mackerel drifters and oar-powered seine boats as a local fishing fleet, it was truly odd to see newcomers – up to thirty Spanish trawlers anchored in Valentia harbour, with a further four or five tied abreast at Knightstown pier for the entire duration of a week-long gale.

However one might shudder today at the thought of unattended youngsters wandering around the dock in the company of foreign seamen, we saw nothing odd about joining these sea-hardened Spanish crews at Knightstown quayside for generous samples of pan-fried *merluza* and black beans in olive oil.

The fact that we dockside urchins spoke no Spanish and that the visiting fishermen spoke no English was no impediment. Sign language is eloquently multilingual when it comes to an invitation to dinner – and what

Knightstown pier awash.

better circumstances than a feast to begin learning a new language? Indeed, what better location for such an exercise than on the open deck of a ship, flying a national flag that was a replica of the red and yellow of the Valentia football team? If we were really lucky, an occasional orange – the first that we had seen in our post-war lives – might be on offer, and besides, the thrill of standing on a real ship's deck was quite a satisfying upgrade from our periwinkle boats of yore and from our daily adventures in the rowing and sailing, and outboard-powered punts of the Cable Station. It was also a part of our continuing education for island life.

There were some entrepreneurial skills to be learned from the Spaniards, too. These seamen did not have a peseta, and they certainly did not have a penny of Irish currency, but they had commodities that were readily marketable. *Terry* and *Tres Copas* brandy could be had for a few shillings, and – slightly later in our campaign – there was a ready opportunity for onward sale to certain local publicans who might not be above slipping it onwards again – at top price – to an inebriated client at a late hour.

But the oddest commodities available in this early international market were ladies' silk stockings. Such goods were not available in the environs of South Kerry; the consequent demand was high, and – notwithstanding the attentions of an occasional customs officer – many a good, duty-free deal was struck at the head of Knightstown pier.

The sin of Tax Avoidance on Imported Goods had not been specifically included in the many admonitions of my catechism lessons, but another early religious crisis came my way that would – for some time – cloud the weekly attendances at Sunday Mass and Holy Communion – which were *de rigueur* under Mom's jurisdiction. And it had nothing to do with ladies' stockings or duty-free brandy; it had all to do with Mrs Cahill's strawberries.

An occasional, weekend sleepover in my Aunt Maureen's home in Knightstown was a special treat that gave me the opportunity to play with another friend and contemporary, Don Cahill. He lived only a few doors away, and we could pop up or down the connecting back lane in a matter of seconds.

One Sunday morning, it was my turn to visit Don, so I headed off early to his house for some playtime before my morning appointment to join Mom at the church for mass. Strawberries! Mrs Cahill's back garden had a wealth of luscious strawberries lining the pathway. I had one. I had two. I had two dozen. Maybe it was two hundred. It was a veritable feast, and when I was fully satisfied, I met Don as planned, and we had our games until mass time.

Mom always occupied the front right-hand seat of the church – not an inconspicuous place – but I made it in time and slid in beside her. All went well until the communion bell rang, and suddenly the enormity of my morning's activity dawned on me: I could not go to Holy Communion because I had stolen strawberries and had also broken the 'fasting from midnight' rule; I couldn't *not* go to Holy Communion because Mom – and Dr McKenna and all the other pillars of Valentia society in the seats behind me, and every soldier of the army contingent in the rows to our left, and all the sailors from the Irish Navy vessel, *Muirchú*, who had dutifully trooped into mass – would know that I had committed some terrible sin.

I had only minutes to consider the implications of my thievery and make a hasty calculation: the Wrath of God and the Fires of Hell were – I hoped – quite far away in the hereafter; the wrath of Mom would be here and now and imminent. It was a 'no contest' situation; I loaded another ton of Catholic guilt on my ten-year-old shoulders and headed up to receive Holy Communion on a bellyful of stolen strawberries.

4

'THE SEM'

Secondary education was always hard to come by in Valentia. Prior to the construction of the Valentia Bridge in 1970, and the ensuing bus services, the only local route to knowledge was an open ferry boat to Renard Point and a three-mile bike ride to the Christian Brothers or the Presentation Convent in Cahersiveen – with the same prospect in reverse in the evening, wet or dry, calm or windy.

This quest for education precipitated the dispersal of our Musketeer group: Dublin would soon claim the two girls in our circle; Colin would head to a seaman's cadet school and to the worldwide seafaring career that this would ultimately entail; Ronnie, we believed, took a route that would lead him to Woomera Rocket Range in Australia, and we would see him no more; John would pursue – and follow right through – a career in cine and TV production; and Adrian alone would brave the local elements by bike and ferry to attend 'The Brothers' in Cahersiveen. I was one of the few islanders of my generation who went as a boarder to St Brendan's Seminary in Killarney – better known as 'The Sem'.

That was September of 1947. For some, it is remembered as the sombre month in which three hundred South Kerry men and youths left Cahersiveen railway station on the emigration trail to England. For me, even if my departure was from Valentia Harbour station rather than Cahersiveen, and en route only to Killarney, it seemed equally distant – and equally dismal.

But I was lucky in my companions there. Two years my senior was fellow islander John O'Connell, and a year earlier still was Paddy Reidy, and I owe them much for saving me from the various rituals, 'hairy bellies' and 'baptisms' that awaited Sem newcomers – or 'plebs' as we were then labelled. It was a precious salvation, as such bullying was not just physical, but mental too. One unfortunate contemporary pleb of less-than-robust constitution and with a serious perspiration problem was – with appropriate ceremonial references to scripture – promptly 'baptised' 'Sick of the Palsy', and he was known thereafter as 'Sick'.

The Sem's South Kerry Group in 1948. I'm in the front row, kneeling, second from left.

If continuing education was my quest, it was an elusive one, as my next academic hurdle, the Intermediate Examination ('Inter Cert') of 1949, registered a failure of some distinction. Some sixty years later – in May 2005 – when first toying with the idea of writing a memoir, and seeking to review the dearth of my scholarly achievements, I telephoned the Secretary of the Sem, looking for my results in that 1949 exam. She could hardly contain her amazement: 'What on earth do you want that for?' was her startled exclamation, knowing that after some five decades, I was hardly writing a CV for a job application. But she dug it up – warts and all.

On a relatively recent April afternoon, I strolled, unattended and unquestioned, through the silent, echoing corridors of the Sem, which is now a day school. The same notice board where I had read that disastrous 1949 exam result was still in the same place and still gave me the same shudders. The oratory – where I had offered many belated, fruitless novenas for scholarly success – was closed, so I could not go in and now offer a few Hail Marys in atonement for my presumptuous expectations of an examination miracle. The ivy had climbed well above and beyond the windows of the study hall where, instead of studying, I read every rag-tag, dog-eared, Wild West paperback that the day-boys could smuggle in to me, and where the whistle of the evening train, bound for the Farranfore connection to Cahersiveen and Valentia harbour, would remind me to cross another day off the countdown to holidays. The windows of the dormitory – where, for the final few pre-examination weeks, I would arise at dawn's light to try to make study-time amends for a year of idleness – looked smaller than I had remembered. I walked by what used to be the 2A classroom, remembering my dismal 58/250 result in History, and recalling how our History and Geography teacher would stride into that room, proclaim 'Beidh Éire fós ag Cáit Ní Dhuíbhir', and then gaze out through the window in silence for the full duration of the class!

That classroom silence suited me at the time. Apart from my own well-established disregard for ancient Irish history, the more recent past had also been a touchy subject in the family circle. And for good reason: I had an English grandfather on one side, and, on the other side, a couple of Irish granduncles who, in their time, had been 'on the run' from somebody or other.

If only that teacher had launched into a project on the American West, I would gladly have trekked and ridden and paddled along with every mile of the Lewis and Clark expedition of 1803 from St Louis, Missouri, to the plains of the Sioux nation, to the headwaters of the Missouri River in Montana and across the Rocky Mountains to the Pacific coast of Oregon – and back. But he didn't. He just stared out of the window and said, 'Beidh Éire fós ag Cáit Ní Dhuíbhir.'

One particular memory was unaltered by that recent April visit. The panoramic photo of the entire college complement of students and teachers – 'Year 48/49' – hanging in the long corridor was a window into a time-warp. For a moment, its characters had not changed, had not moved on to great things, had not died. For a moment, they were still tender teenagers, ready – if fearful – to troop into Jackeen's class for Latin and Greek; ready – if terrified – to face trig, algebra and allied hardships; ready – *and eager* – to cram into the science lab for Thadgo's wildly exciting topics; or happy in classroom 2A to welcome the stimulating English class of Danny Long. But mostly, the photo confirmed that it was not all just a distant, childhood hallucination; I was there in the midst of it all – if only in the back row – a poor, hungry-looking, scholar of the 1940s.

Hungry-looking, perhaps, but it's not that I was starved; I must have been born that way, because I was forever the recipient of various childhood tonics and treatments. Happily, prior to my Sem years, I had outgrown the 'chest complaint' that called for a long-nosed kettle on a bedroom fire spewing medication-laden steam into my airways. But even into my teenage years, 'Doctor Jessel's Tablets' were good for something-or-other, 'Parrish's Food' was good for something else, and that dreadful, iodine-coloured stuff had to be sucked through a straw or it would blacken every tooth.

Cod-liver-oil capsules were, allegedly, 'very good for the bones'. In the Sem, I also found them really excellent for something else – slipping one into someone's tea, so that when the capsule promptly dissolved and the blob of oil was released, the inattentive tea-gulper would get a palate-full of the foulest taste on earth!

General complaints about food at the Sem seem to have surfaced in every generation. I have no such argument. If anything, the school's once-weekly Irish stew is still high in my overall food ratings, equal to other landmark meals around the world: Best 'Irish' Breakfast – the Wembley Hilton Hotel; Best Prime Rib of Beef – the Lamplighter Restaurant, Butte, Montana; Best Chicken Sandwich – the Old Ground Hotel, Ennis; Best Tiramisu dessert – the Museum of Modern Art in San Francisco; Best Irish Stew – the Sem!

Indeed, in solid defence of the Sem's culinary services, that photo of 'Year 48/49' shows some two hundred and twelve rather fit boys, with no evidence of malnutrition, and, more importantly, no trace of the overweight and obesity problems that seem to bedevil today's scholars to the point of a national emergency.

We did not have many gooey buns in the Sem in the 1940s, but I do remember a can of sticky sweets, and I still have a fading scar on the index finger of my right hand as a memento of that.

It was Retreat Week – when self-mortification was the buzz-word of every sermon at every daily mass and prayer session. Not being overly impressed by self-mortification matters, I kept a secret stash of canned sweets as my lifesaver – that is, until I lacerated my finger in an overzealous assault on the can. A sick-bay visit followed; and a lie followed that, because I could not admit to enjoying sticky sweets during Retreat Week. But my lie and my overindulgence were appropriately punished when flies and insects got into my unattended, open can, spoiling the remaining contents.

I did not realise in 1947 that the Sem had serious aspirations of being a seminary for clerical vocations, and I don't believe that my being sent there resulted from any such ulterior motive. But the incentives for holiness there were legion: daily mass and a plethora of prayer appointments in the oratory were not the only spiritual seeds; altar boy duty in the nearby St Mary's Cathedral was another function.

I enjoyed this diversion; it was an escape from some other mundane activity. And if those of us who had no previous experience as altar boys in our home parishes sometimes turned the Latin response, '*Ad deum qui laetificat juventutem meum*', into 'Idiom qui laugh-at-the-cat you went tootem-eum', nobody seemed to notice.

One particular priest on the Cathedral's roster was a much-favoured confessor. In his court, a couple of Hail Marys could readily atone for everything. Even admitting to an occasional bout of youthful masturbation did not incur his ire, whereas other priests – and visiting missionaries in particular – imposed decades of the Rosary or the risk of serious Hell-time for the same 'terrible sin'! If 'shopping around' for the most lenient confessor could be regarded as Market Research, the inevitable queue of would-be penitents outside one particular confessional box surely told its own eloquent story of Customer Satisfaction!

But our real favourite in the Cathedral was neither cleric nor confessor, but Mr O'Malley, the groundsman. A total football fanatic, he must have attended every Munster Football Final and every All-Ireland that Kerry ever played, and he could hold us enthralled with his vivid kick-by-kick and blow-by-blow account of them all. Long-time Kerry goalkeeper, Dan O'Keefe, was Mr O'Malley's hero. He was mine too, as he had dominated the Kerry goal-line for more than my entire life span of fourteen years. Still ringing in my ears some seven decades later is Mr O'Malley's vivid vision of the fabled 'Danno' diving across *the full width of the goal*' to save some vital shot *with the very nails of his fingers!*' As a graphic reconstruction, it was more visible, more detailed, more eloquent, and much more memorable than any modern TV replay or Hawk-Eye examination.

In light of latter-day clerical revelations, it's worth noting that the Sem, with its priest-dominated staff, never incurred even a whisper of child abuse – other than the normal incentives for successful studies in the shape of the bamboo canes of some teachers and the triceps-pinching penchant of others. These physical reprimands were a part of the package, and were soon and easily forgotten, but some less visible internal injuries from public humiliation by vicious sarcasm have not healed.

'How would a Valentia man know left from right?' was the lash I got when I about-turned to the left instead of to the right during one cleric's extreme ventures into our Physical Education. Equally upsetting to this day is the fact that although I had already suffered enough in having all my wretched teeth filled by Dentist Sheehan in Cahersiveen in preparation for my Sem sojourn, I was obliged nonetheless to visit the college-appointed dentist in Killarney, who drilled out and re-filled the lot.

A much-envied student from Glenfesk was the proud owner of a 'Biro' ballpoint pen - the first one that any of us had ever seen. What a revolution, I thought! What a design-leap from my old fountain pen that oozed ink and had to be re-filled every couple of days. And what wonderful blue ink, this ballpoint stuff – useful for making instant, indelible laundry ID tags, far superior to those that had taken Dad many careful hours of work with black Indian ink and a steel-nib pen – itself not far removed from the quills of even earlier days. 'Des Lavelle 738' looked much better in blue, as my sack of underwear offerings wended its way to some laundry somewhere.

Dad spent many hours marking my school clothes with indelible laundry ID tags.
He is pictured here with Rinty and me in the 1950s.

But my old fountain pen had its memorable hours too, particularly when I wrote an English essay entirely in green ink. I still don't know why the colour green made our normally sanguine English teacher, Danny Long, so distressed. Blue ink, black ink, green ink, what did it matter so long as the essays and the topics were good?

The only other occasion when I noted similar upset in this good priest was when I met him again in the 1970s, shortly after the publication of Patrick Kennelly's book, *Sausages for Tuesday*, which relates that the boys of 'St Andrew's' – a thinly disguised St Brendan's Seminary – were fraternising rather intimately with the college's maids.

'Ye weren't really fornicating with the maids?' asked my distressed, long-retired teacher.

'No,' I could truthfully reply. But his query and his obvious concern left me wondering what exciting collateral educational opportunities I may have missed by quitting formal education to go to work at age sixteen.

Fifty years after I had quit, in April 1990, the question of education – secondary, or, indeed, primary – would rear its head in the public press and radio, with reports of widespread illiteracy. A simple poster of that time, originating in Cahersiveen, to advertise the Valentia 10km road race, labelled the Juvenile sector as 'Junivelle'.

Related topics still appear on occasion: *The Irish Times* – January 2017, September 2019 and April 2021 – covered the question of adult literacy again and set me thinking about the real difficulties of the English language if someone has missed out on the confusing basics.

adult literacy

and so deer teecher teech me how to spell
so abc may leed to zee as well
i no i kinda one time did that stuff
but that was then and now tis not enuff

i need to put more lerning in my hed
and try to reed the stuff I never red
at leest to match the others of my age
and not to quit at one line down the page

to rite the letters that I never rote
to mark the ballet paper for my vote
the things they lerned whiled I was skippin class
to reed the drivin test and maybe pass

id like to rite a letter to my mom
to tell her she was rite and I was rong
i no its late kos shees not here today
but still sheed no bout what I try to say

id say deer mom I love you do you heer
im getting help ill make it never feer
im tryin now to make you proud as hell
and so deer teecher teech me how to spell

Indeed, whatever the educational opportunities of the Sem era, be they real or imagined, wasted or otherwise, this mediocre scholar was destined never to feature in the career statistics that are the *real* yardstick of the Sem's overall performance. Allegedly, the crop of two hundred and twelve boys in that 'Year 48/49' photo yielded sixty priests and two bishops!

5

THE JOB

I joined the Western Union Telegraph Company on Valentia Island on 1 February 1950 at the tender age of sixteen years – and promptly labelled my august employment 'The Job', in a personal rebellion against the stuffiness and snobbery that went with the senior gentry of the Cable Station establishment.

Status they certainly had. Here, in the extremities of coastal Kerry, stood this industry of worldwide importance, linking the telegraph outlets of Europe with their counterparts in Canada and the United States. To this quest in the 1850s had come international engineers, international financiers and international sea captains, working together to achieve something impossible – laying a telegraph cable on the seabed across the Atlantic Ocean to join the two continents.

Those glorious pioneering years waxed and waned; early cable failures – disaster enough to quench any zeal – were eventually overcome; fragile, febrile contact was established; Valentia's western clifftop location at Foilhammerum, where the first successful message exchange occurred in 1868, was eventually abandoned in favour of Knightstown, and a newly constructed cable office and related staff dwellings soon graced the impressive waterfront site which they still occupy today. The fruits of the 1857

Western Union Telegraph Company staff, including retirees, in the 1950s.

visionaries' foresight were finally a fact of Knightstown life.

I welcomed the idea of going to work in the Cable Station. As a status symbol of the 1950s, it was better to be a working man than a schoolboy – as my Musketeer contemporaries still were. As a further status symbol, it was better to be working in the Cable Station than anywhere else, because the sacred phrase, 'a permanent, pensionable job', was on every advisor's lips. Besides, collecting a weekly wage of £2.15 – itself the price of a splendid suit from the travelling 'Fifty Shilling Tailors' salesmen of subsequent years – was a more attractive option than going back to the 'Sem' to face another – and possibly even less successful – attempt at the Inter Cert exam again at year's end.

My duties would be in the Engine Room where three diesel generators and a great room full of storage batteries provided electricity for the entire station – telegraph operations, domestic power and public lighting for the twenty-three dwellings and their extensive grounds.

Joining the Engine Room staff – or Plant Maintenance Electricians, to give us our full title – may have been regarded as an inferior posting to that of

Telegraph Operator, and certainly commanded lower wages and conditions, one such condition being that we, as distinct from the telegraph operators, did not merit the occupancy of a rent-free Cable Station dwelling house as part of our employment. This distinction hardly mattered to me at the time; I was still living with Mom and Dad – my now-recognised grandparents. Nor did the distinction matter greatly in 1956 when marriage and the need of accommodation brought me no free housing but saw me quite content to pay a rent of £4 per quarter for the unfurnished No.15, Cable Station.

ESB poles being delivered at Knightstown pier, heralding the arrival on the island of the Electricity Supply Board's rural electrification scheme.

Meanwhile, I was happy to soak up the necessary practical skills – engine and generator maintenance, workshop practices, and industrial and domestic electrical installation. As of yore, these skills were quite ahead of the times in Valentia; the Electricity Supply Board's rural electrification scheme would not reach us until 1959 when the *M.V. Galtee* docked at Knightstown harbour with the first cargo of poles and equipment.

The Valentia Cable Station was already almost one hundred years in existence at this stage, and while its peak employment of two hundred and forty-two staff in the more manual period of 1921 had promptly faded thereafter, the thirty remaining employees of 1950–60 still constituted an odd selection of mankind to find in the backwoods of County Kerry. Most of the elders were immigrants – largely from England – who, though having spent all their working lives on Valentia, never quite integrated and could scarcely wait for retirement to head back to the UK, to warmer climes or to pastures new.

There were many Freemasons amongst this immigrant group. They were rather a mystery to those of us in the Catholic community, and the secrecy of their meetings and procedures gave the topic rather more importance than it ultimately deserved. But curiosity led me to buy a book, *Darkness Visible* (Walton Hannah, Augustinian Press, London, 1952), to see what this Freemasonry was all about. 'Handy reading for the nightshift on The Job,' I thought. But I never got past Chapter One. In my absence, someone completely mutilated the book beyond redemption, tore it apart, page by page! Had it simply been stolen, the loss of the book would have been a mystery, nothing more. But its total destruction was something else; it was a message. And in the lower echelons of the Cable Station's 'permanent, pensionable employment', I was inclined to accept such an initial – if cryptic – message, rather than persevere and incur a possible, later, more concrete warning of some sort.

I never found out who destroyed that book. Was it a Freemason, in preservation of the precious signs, symbols and 'secrets' of Ireland's 47,000 Masons of that 1950s period? Or was it some extreme Catholic, concerned that I might join the Masonic Lodge and suffer an inevitable excommunication as first mandated by Pope Clement XII's Encyclical, *In Eminenti,* of 1738? In any case, I did not replace the mutilated book. Nor did I see the title again for half a century until the desperation of a week of bad weather in San Francisco in January 2008 prompted me to catch up on my unfinished reading, and the library of West Portal found me a well-thumbed 1955 edition of the same controversial *Darkness Visible* that had so upset that Valentia extremist of yore.

Thus, some fifty years later, I completed my reading of this small, red-covered, 231-page, hardback publication – without, I might add, discovering any particular exposé of the Freemasons' 'secrets', or constituting any particular additional hazard to my immortal soul.

'The Job' led to another peculiar event in the same 1950s era. My nightshift duties provided for a supper hour at 1am, and since home was only fifty yards away, this break was spent listening to late-night radio rather than partaking in any serious dining. 'Surfing' a radio dial at that time of night in the 1950s offered little besides a few international short-wave stations. But Radio Moscow was one such broadcaster, and its mixture of entertainment and commentary in the English language attracted my attention frequently – so frequently that I even wrote a letter to the station, praising its contribution to my night-time hours.

Radio Moscow must have read my letter over the air, because one morning, shortly afterwards, I was accosted in the street by the local parish priest.

'I hear you've been listening to Radio Moscow,' he said sombrely. I was struck speechless and brainless by the shock realisation that some Big Brother was out there, watching, listening – and interpreting my late-night radio entertainment as an involvement in Communist propaganda. Or worse! Was the parish priest himself the Radio Moscow listener? Or was it one Denis Moynihan, then Bishop of Kerry? Or was it some surveillance unit of the Vatican State of Pius XII? True, it was the Cold War era. True, Senator Joseph McCarthy was at the height of his paranoid witch-hunt for 'Communist sympathisers' under every American bed. But was the paranoia also much closer to home?

For better or worse, I remember not one other word of that morning's discussion with the disapproving priest, but if subsequent 1am supper breaks brought me Radio Moscow or AFN (the American Forces Network), or anything in between, I wrote no letters about it.

In some other peculiar frame of mind, in the same period, I joined the FCA – a part-time civilian army supplement. As a committed pacifist, then and now, who abhors war, warmongers, capital punishment and related barbarism, I hardly proposed to 'lay down my life for my country' in the light of someone else's perceived fear of catastrophic world domination. But my odd venture bothered nobody; a rather common belief at that time was that a valid, logical motive for joining the FCA was the acquisition of a free uniform, a heavy overcoat, and a pair of substantial boots!

Those were not my reasons. If, perhaps, my real reason for joining the force was as whimsical as reliving the memories of childhood years when we Musketeers mimicked the 'square-bashing' and manoeuvres of our military neighbours in the Valentia army garrison, my eventual reason for resigning was equally trivial. I soon concluded that I wasn't really cut out for the FCA as exemplified by the rather explicit language emanating from a drill sergeant in Kilworth Camp when some unfortunate private misinterpreted his instruction: 'Soldier, am I giving you an order or am I whistling out through my arse?'

Apart from such verbal expressions not common in the hallowed halls of

With my FCA colleagues. I'm in the centre of the back row.

the Cable Station, I did learn three skills in the FCA – two of them useful, one not. I learned to stand erect, to walk tall, and to hit a bulls-eye consistently with a .303 Lee-Enfield rifle at 300 yards.

The useful lessons were put to some good use in the same era – with the Valentia Pipe Band! Here was an organisation that waxed and waned over generations and, in the throes of one such renaissance in the 1960s, needed a Drum Major to take the lead. Tall enough, and able to march with the best, I got the duty – and a tartan sash, a busby and a noble staff. The piping of this renaissance was excellent, reaching a climax in a competition in Limerick's Thomond Park. My order of 'Ready, Rolls, One, Two!' needed no amplification; it might have been heard as far away as Rathkeale! And the terrace applause when we were judged trophy winners was easily the equivalent of any modern Munster/Leinster rugby encounter.

It went a bit to our heads – some heads anyhow – and enthusiastic, if

Tall enough, and able to march with the best, I got the duty of Drum Major with the Valentia Pipe Band.

deteriorating, celebratory encores were performed en route home anywhere that had a main street. Fortunately, some hamlets along the way had front gardens rather than shop windows, and when my tossed staff had to be retrieved from a blackthorn bush, I decided to call it a day.

In any event, I had other, real, work-related interests to occupy my time, by night or by day. A hunger for yet more electrical and mechanical theory in my work training led me to undertake a 1950s-style version of Continuing Education – a correspondence course with the fine title of Electrical Engineering. Humble though it was, it constituted another valuable strand of enlightenment, another satisfying string to my bow, another layer of security in my 'permanent, pensionable' job.

Unfortunately, Valentia's statistics did not really support many aspirations for permanence or security. The island's population was in free-fall through emigration; the 2,920 souls of the 1841 census had dropped to 2,240 in 1861, and to 1,015 in 1951. The concurrent drop in Cable Station staff had little to do with local conditions; rather, it was a direct result of the advancing technology and automation of the 1920s, which saw the staff numbers fall from two hundred to a few dozen.

However, further forces were poised to interfere with Valentia's cable industry. Nobody had foreseen the massive expansion of international fishing power that would hit the Irish Continental Shelf at the conclusion of the Second World War. In earlier times, if a fisherman's nets became snagged on undersea telegraph cables, he would invariably lose those nets. But bigger marine engines and substantial post-war investment in European fishing fleets changed all this; now it was the nets that were sacrosanct, not the cables, and widespread cable damage ensued. Not that it was difficult to damage them; large portions of the cable were already quite old, and the

Specialist cable ships such as the *Edouard Suenson* were required to repair damaged undersea cables.

costs of specialist cable ships – the *Lord Kelvin*, the *Marie Louise Mackay*, the *John W. Mackay*, the *Edouard Suenson*, the *Monarch*, the *Poolster*, the *Cyrus Field* – to repair the repeated damage mounted daily.

Satellite communications were coming on stream too, but the real nails in the Valentia coffin were in the form of new transatlantic cables from Scotland to North America that were laid by a European consortium in the 1950s and ploughed into the safety of the seabed. Furthermore, these were *telephone* cables, and could take many times more simultaneous traffic signals than Valentia's originals. Western Union promptly rerouted its telegraphic communications through these new cables, and by 1966, with the closure of the Cable Station, there were only 874 people left on Valentia Island.

So, after sixteen years and three days, my 'permanent, pensionable' job was gone, and I had a 'Notice to Quit' in my hand. On the notepaper of Western Union International Inc, it read:

6th January 1966

Dear Mr. Lavelle,

With the closure of the Valentia Cable Station on February 3rd I hereby give you notice that you are required to vacate the house which you occupy by virtue of your employment with this Company on that date.

Yours truly,
W.D. Breslin
Station Superintendent

Even though the writing had been on the wall, it was a shock to see so many families disrupted – to see some old friends and workmates destined

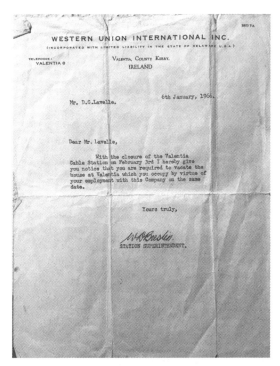

Left: After sixteen years and three days, my 'permanent, pensionable' job was gone, and I had this 'Notice to Quit' in my hand.

Below: Cable station children impacted by the 1966 closure. Even though the writing had been on the wall, it was a shock to see so many families disrupted.

to depart Valentia to seek a living elsewhere. There were some limited job opportunities on offer with the Western Union's London offices at 22 Great Winchester Street, and some would accept those. Others would find work where their technical and communications skills were valuable. Some would opt to remain in Valentia.

However, if I had never previously heard of anyone losing a 'permanent, pensionable' job, neither had I ever heard of 'Redundancy Money'. And all of a sudden, I had a redundancy payment of £600 in my hand. £600! It was a fortune in 1966, and it merited careful handling.

In common with some of my Engine Room colleagues, I could readily go freelancing locally in domestic electrical installation work that followed the ESB's ongoing local electrical connections since Christmas 1959. Those of us among the Engine Room staff were well qualified to do so, and we did not have to begin on the same rung as another well-publicised entrepreneur who – when the rural electrification reached his area – wrote to the ESB:

> Dear Sir,
> Please send me some booklets and leaflets on how to wire houses and farmyards for the electric current, also send some leaflets on how to treat a person for electric shock....

But I had other ideas. I was still ensconced in my Cable Station house, and being a rent-paying tenant, I could disregard the Station Superintendent's futile 'Notice to Quit'. I also had my £600 redundancy money to invest.

I was thirty-two years of age; I had a wife and two daughters. I found a man in Ballybunion who would build me a 26ft boat for £600, and we humorously named her the *Sardana* – after a Catalan folk dance that goes around and around in circles. The die was thus cast for seeking a living in Valentia.

With hindsight, my lack of awe at the end of the cable era was odd. Likewise, my youthful lack of interest in the magnitude of the Cable Station's international status. I had grown up in its ambience. It had been a part of life for several generations. Thus, for me, there was nothing special about it.

But today, some sixty years and two generations later – and with a new appreciation of things historical – Valentia Cable Station's history, and its still-impressive presence in bricks and mortar, again make international headlines in serious efforts to see both Valentia Island and Hearts Content in Canada accorded World Heritage Site status because of the world-changing communication events that occurred here in 1868, when, at last, a message could cross the Atlantic in minutes or seconds, rather than at the lumbering tempo of a sailing ship.

Likewise, following the 1966 closure, few islanders were interested in the subsequent auction of Cable Station equipment, as various telegraphic antiques of no further practical use were snapped up by knowledgeable, visiting collectors. Today, we must resort to the Valentia Island Heritage Centre (formerly the Knightstown National School) to view some of these unique instruments – on loan to the Valentia exhibition from generous benefactors. Equally – and also in the World Heritage Site quest – we note current plans to create a Cable Interpretative Centre in what was once the foyer and billiard room of the cable offices.

In a related Zoom conference in October 2020, with local speakers in Hearts Content, Newfoundland – where still stands the equivalent Cable Station, once linked to Valentia by that 1868 cable – I was struck by the similarity of the human experiences voiced on both sides of the Atlantic. Like Valentia, Hearts Content had seen a boom-time at the arrival of the cable technicians in the 1860s. Their good wages spread money across a remote coastal extremity, filtering onwards to butcher, baker and tradesman – an economy that collapsed with the 1966 demise of the cable. When one speaker reminisced that local women of that era had depended on the cable staff's laundry requirements to earn a living, it reminded me that in my childhood, a dear old Valentia lady used to walk some four miles on a Monday morning to come to the Cable Station and do Mom's washing in a big wooden tub in the back yard.

6

MARRIAGE

I married – once – at twenty-two years of age, on 8 September 1956. It was a contract that would thrive and endure for fifty-four years until a long illness finally took Pat from me on 11 March 2010.

Our marriage was the culmination of a long and arduous courtship – long in the sense that it went on for five years, and arduous in the sense that Patricia O'Neill lived in the mainland town of Cahersiveen and I lived on the island of Valentia – with the wide, wild waters of Valentia harbour in between. True, there was a Knightstown-based ferry service, but apart from a few fixed times, the mail ferry, the creamery ferry, or the train ferry in pre-1960 days, the Knightstown/Renard ferry service marched to its own day-time drum, and did not facilitate late-night travellers, cinemagoers, mainland revellers or anyone who wanted to come and go in the small hours.

The obvious way around all this was to use one's own rowing boat, and to travel in twos or threes and share the labours of launching the vessel in Valentia, pulling it up clear of the tide at Renard pier, re-launching it in the dawn of the morning and rowing home. The rougher the weather, the tougher the experience, and being encumbered with a cargo of two or three bicycles laid across the gunwales of a punt was quite a long step from ferrying a childhood cargo of periwinkles along the beach in a toy boat.

'I row 500 miles to see the girl I love' was the rather extravagant head-line in the *Sunday Review* of 26 March 1961, when I wrote a feature on the related – or possibly exaggerated – hardships of a cross-channel romance.

The absolute transport luxury of these outings, and the only way to reach Cahersiveen and get home – without two layers of perspiration – was to leave Valentia on the last of the scheduled evening ferry services, which was at about 6.30pm, take ourselves and our bicycles on the final train of the day to Cahersiveen, and have a freelance oarsman, Seán Casey, meet us with his own rowing boat at Renard for the return trip at some appointed late hour.

The downside of this arrangement was that there was only one meeting place at Renard – the Point House pub. A further downside was that – as immortalised in amendments to that local ditty, 'The Waters That Flow Round Valentia' – a 'liking for Guinness's stout' could often result in some-one's considerable reluctance to quit the said facility. The ferryman, perhaps, did not have to go to work the following morning; others frequently did – at 6am!

Other marine escapades, like visiting Spanish trawlers at the harbour, did not end with schooldays, teenage or marriage. Nor did such ventures any longer relate to brandy or similar commodities. In fact, many Spanish skippers and crew – Eusebio from San Sebastian, Patchi-the-Basque, Tuto Rodriguez from Vigo – were old friends at this stage, and visiting them on their ships was a normal part of an international relationship.

But one early visit to a Spanish trawler, on 27 November 1954, nearly put a stop to our gallop and almost saw me under house-arrest by Mom. The date is better remembered locally as the November night when the local trawler, Christy Shea's *Ros Airgead*, went aground in a westerly gale on the White Strand.

In ideal conditions earlier that afternoon, together with my colleague and co-worker, Nealie Donovan, I set out from Valentia in a naomhóg to visit the Spanish trawler, *H. Puebla*, that was at anchor in Valentia harbour. Onboard hospitality was as generous as ever and we dined well on pan-fried hake and Spanish bread rolls, followed by tinned peaches and tar-strong coffee with sweetened condensed milk. Conversation and card games led one hour into the next until it was time to go home.

However, that was the end of the fun. When we came up on deck, a veritable storm was blowing – force 9 or more – and there was no way that we could even attempt to board the naomhóg, much less row it ashore in the teeth of the wind. We were stuck, with no option but to sit it out.

And other complications were also in train. The local '50-footer', *Ros Airgead*, having set out from Knightstown in darkness and blinding rain to head upriver to the shelter of Cahersiveen, did not make it; she missed the river mouth by half a mile, luckily missed the Passage Rock and its surrounding teeth, and ran aground on the solid sand of the White Strand. Now the Valentia lifeboat was involved, and this exacerbated our position. From the bridge of the *H. Puebla*, we could see and hear the two maroons summoning the lifeboat crew at Knightstown. On the trawler's crackling radio, we gathered what was going on. But there was no way our folk at home would be party to all this information. Nor was there any way we could inform them. And I knew that Mom, on hearing the lifeboat maroons, would typically assume the worst: Donovan and I were missing in the storm or already drowned.... Prayers for the dead were probably being recited.

Some lull eventually came before the November dawn, and we managed to board the naomhóg and head for home into the teeth of the wind. It was the toughest test of our lives – two inches forward, one inch back, until we reached the welcoming gravel of Knightstown beach in an exhausted state. There I was happy to fall down and kiss the very stones where many a periwinkle-boat voyage had made a similarly successful landfall under similar, relative duress of weather full twenty years previously.

The postscript to the event was that the *Ros Airgead* was subsequently re-floated on a later tide and was soon back to normal operations, but it was quite a long time before normality returned to my grandmother's mindset regarding my nautical activities.

In a contrasting vote of confidence, Pat – then girlfriend; later, wife, mother and grandmother – never had any such reservations about my sea-faring pursuits. She lost no sleep on my account even throughout my subsequent years of commercial boating or lifeboat services in the most foul sea conditions. Perhaps our long association with water-safety procedures and classes added that measure of confidence.

Luckily, Valentia harbour is not subject to much fog – perhaps only some nine days of it per year. In any case, Valentia fogs are seldom 'pea-soupers', and a compass-less, radar-less punt of the 1950s could normally expect a successful harbour crossing. Confidently, in the pre-dawn of a quiet, calm summer's night in 1954, with just a hint of fog, I set out with Seán Casey on one such homeward journey from Renard pier – only to be enveloped within minutes in a cloud of zero visibility! It was guesswork from here on, pausing occasionally to try to glean a clue from onshore noises. There were none. We were hopelessly lost on a mirror-calm sea.

After an hour, we found land. If this was Valentia, there should have been a road just above the beach – but there was no road. We walked the beach in one direction and recognised nothing. We walked the beach in the other direction, and within minutes encountered the Renard pier of our recent departure. Chastened, a lesson learned, we sat, and, more wisely, waited till the fog lifted.

Nonetheless, undaunted and unfazed by fog, wind or rain, we would answer the call of Cahersiveen cinema and that of the Iveragh Ballroom. Even more distant calls would be answered, too. Pat, single or married, would follow the music to the end of the earth – the end of the county, anyhow, as we once braved a trip on a Lambretta scooter to Ballybunion at the other extremity of Kerry to dance to Victor Sylvester and his Orchestra.

Sometimes, in those early days, we Valentia revellers travelled in groups – big-spenders, 1950s style – in Paty Sheehy's Cahersiveen taxi, to the Oscar Ballroom in Castlemaine, the Oisín Ballroom in Killorglin or the Emer in Glenbeigh, to dance until four in the morning to the music of Jimmy Rohan, Denis Cronin and Mick Delahunty. We went to a circus in Killorglin once – a bunch of penniless Valentia heroes – and spent our fortune on the best seats. In the course of the evening, there was some kind of raffle, with the prize being a refund of the entry-ticket price. Luckily, I won the prize; otherwise, I would not have had the means to leave Valentia again for a fortnight!

'My wife should be down on her knees, thanking God for how well she married' was somebody else's line that I often tossed about when good company induced jokes and banter. Pat, of course, would counter with the inevitable truth that I was the one who did all the pursuit and proposed marriage to her hundreds of times – almost from our first meeting on an excursion train returning from the Munster Final in Killarney.

Strangely, I remember only two proposals: one, a rather unsuccessful try, was admittedly a very poorly chosen moment – not quite while she was enjoying romantic dance music on a graceful cruise ship beneath a million Pacific Ocean stars, but when she was in the throes of seasickness on the after-deck of a smelly Cahersiveen trawler, the *Naomh Cáit*, lurching its way home from a Dingle regatta in the teeth of a westerly gale!

The final proposal – which she could have refused, but didn't – came with a £25 ring, on the top deck of Hook Head lighthouse in the county of Wexford.

On 8 September 1956, we married in Cork city. For Kerry folk of that era, it was probably the equivalent of going to Hawaii for the nuptials of today! Bizarrely, my parents did not attend even though they were no farther away than Hook Head, County Wexford. If their absence was ever explained to me at the time, I don't remember the details. It may have been that an inspection of Hook Head lighthouse was foisted upon my father at short notice.

It doesn't matter now – and it didn't matter then. In the company of many O'Neills, and best man, Nealie Donovan, we had a wonderful wedding with fervent toasts in lemonade and Club Orange.

The pub scene was never my focus then; I was always literally driven to tears in the smoke-filled pub atmosphere. Many years later, when I first encountered smoke-free pubs in San Francisco, I thought: 'What a splendid concept; pity it could never happen in Ireland.' In fact, so certain was I that it *could not* happen in Ireland, that I shouted a rash pledge from the rooftops: if Irish pubs ever became smoke-free, I would become an accomplished drunkard! But I failed in that pledge; if I have one pint of Guinness, I may be a candidate for the title of Life and Soul of the Party; if I have two pints, I fall asleep.

But yes, whatever the date, dance floors still called. One extreme outing saw Pat and myself 'leading the floor' in The Bridge Bar in Portmagee in December 2000. The bar was full, but nobody joined us. For the duration of a splendid Johnny Cash number, we had the floor to ourselves. Little wonder: I had a great black eye and a bandage the size of half a turban on my forehead – the aftermath of one of many skin grafts arising from all that childhood sunburn of the 1940s. This particular 'turban' originated in Dublin's Mount Carmel Hospital when a graft from my right thigh eventually graced my troublesome forehead. But there were many other 'forehead episodes' over the years, involving stays at a variety of hospitals. Finally, in September 2010, during a stay at the University Hospital, Cork, new grafts – taken from both sides of my chest – filled my forehead vacancy, and provided a repair that has served well to 2021 – and, I hope, far beyond.

That extreme facial accessory, temporarily held in place with 'bolster' bandage sewn to my skin, certainly drew aghast glances and questions anew from colleague and stranger alike whom I met on the terra firma of Ireland, but – in a strange exposé of international or professional psyche – it drew not a glance or a comment from the Swedish Captain and First Officer of a cruise ship I was piloting a few days later.

In any event, by then I was quite inured to reaction, comment, commiseration – or the lack of it – since a particular early graft, sourced behind my left ear in 'The Bons' in Cork spurred me to think of the Dutch artist, M.C. Escher, and ponder...

Escher

Remember an artist named Escher,
Who etched some incredible things.
His fishes and birds-of-a-feather
All merged till the fishes grew wings.
His rivers ran uphill for ever.
His columns were in the wrong place.
It would not surprise if my ears were my eyes,
And the back of my head was my face.

In the 1950s, the cost of conducting a five-year romance over the telephone could be regarded as a financial incentive to marriage. With no Vodafone, Three, Eir or Tesco Mobile clamouring for my business, the monopolistic Department of Posts & Telegraphs collected a goodly portion of my humble wage packet via the one available local phone in the Cable Station office – 'Valentia 8' – due to many long-duration calls to a certain girl named Patricia O'Neill at 'Cahersiveen 18'.

Marriage saved all that. And there were further eventual savings and much more comfort available when we finally got the then *luxury* of our own phone – 'Valentia 24' – in our No. 15 Cable Terrace home. After that, international calls could sometimes be free, as Cousin May, who worked in a Dublin P&T exchange, would phone us occasionally and offer us (free) connections to anywhere. I don't know that we used her services heavily – if at all. Who in the backwoods of Valentia had any need to make long-distance phone calls in the late 1950s or 1960s? Certainly not us.

Nor indeed, in those early years of marriage, had we any urgent wish for the finer things of domestic life. In our £4-a-quarter house in 1956 we had a bed, a two-ring gas cooker, a kitchen table – homemade by myself – and a kitchen cabinet, similarly 'handcrafted' from the wood of elaborate packing crates that were used to transport telegraph instruments and mechanical

We would finally experience the luxury of our own phone – Valentia 24 – at our number 15 Cable Terrace home.

items from the USA. Even the domestic bath and its related comforts had to come later.

We did have one respectable item, though – a dining-room suite. This was more or less obligatory; it was essential to have 'The Room' right – even if, like in my grandparents' house, it was never used.

And if I was a handyman and a fixer, Pat brought her many skills to the £4-a-quarter house too. Even on a two-ring gas cooker, she could produce meals that the proud owners of many a modern six-ring hob might envy. On a hand-operated sewing machine that had been bought with the savings of ten shillings a week, she could make the girls' clothes from the flannelette off-cuts that were freely available as the dusting and mopping-up cloths of 'The Job'. With lace curtain material, bought wholesale from diver/friend Frank McMahon in Dublin, she could make a First Communion dress that would cost €500 in today's boutiques.

Backwoods or not, social life was adequate indeed in the late 1950s. And again, it related to boating – this time, sailing boats. Thanks to the initiatives of Tom Shortt, a boat club with the rather ambitious name of 'The Atlantic Sailing Club' grew up in Cahersiveen and Valentia. We never sailed the Atlantic, but with a couple of clincher-built, 14ft, IDRA sailing dinghies and several substantial sailing boats of no particular denomination, we enjoyed much competition and fun. Local regattas once again offered sailing races – something that had not been seen in Valentia harbour for years – and medals of real silver were on offer, some of which are still in the family today.

However, '1st Sailing Boat, Valentia Regatta, 1958' or '2nd Sailing Boat, Valentia Regatta, 1957' or '2nd Sailing Boat, Valentia Regatta, 1961' did not necessarily mean that I was always first or second across the line on my own merits; so haphazard was the handicapping guesswork in the wide variety of non-class boats that I still managed to win a race in an odd, unlikely vessel borrowed from Colonel Uniacke of Glanleam House.

This boat had no name; she was of no classification; her most recent competitive outing had been the Valentia regatta of 1948 under Charles Spring-Rice and Major Bell of Fota Island; and her greatest claim to fame was her propensity to capsize unattended at her moorings. But now – for the sailing club's Harbour Trophy race of 1959 – I sallied forth in her with crewman/cousin Raphael Greene.

The vessel had not been out of the boathouse for years, and Raphael's sole onboard job for the entire race was to bail out the water that was pouring in through every seam – a duty so onerous that he did not see the start, rounding-mark or finishing line. In fact, the 'water-ballast' even helped. In a race through a force 5 sou'wester that saw Tom Shortt's *Mercury* dis-masted and impaled on the Portmagee Perch rock, our mongrel vessel, with her small sail area, thrived where the thoroughbreds failed, and we coasted home in first place – even without the help of the thirty-minute handicap that the compassionate race committee had allocated to our noble ship.

The Harbour Trophy that was in my hands by evening felt like Valentia's equivalent of The America's Cup! Even if that trophy has long since gone wherever trophies go, its accompanying, hallmarked gold and silver medal, '*Harbour Trophy Sailing Race 1959. 1ˢᵗ Sailing Boat*', is none-the-worse for its sixty-odd years.

Oarsman trophies, I have none, though. One session in the Valentia seine boat, *The Shamrock,* pulling on the second oar with 'Jereen J' McCarthy at some now-distant 1950s Valentia regatta was enough. Who beat us on the day, or where we were placed, matters not. My only memory of that regatta is of the chairman, Tady Driscoll, standing on the wall by the then Bank Office on the waterfront and bellowing: 'If the coxswains of the seine boats don't come forward to collect their prize money, we'll bloody-well drink it for them!'

Regattas aside, Pat and I – and Nero, our cocker spaniel – did much leisure sailing. The birth of our daughter, Céline, in 1959, did not hamper this in the least. Much as one may shudder today at the thought, the infant's carry-cot was dutifully loaded athwartships on the flat flooring beneath the helm, and away we sailed, with the uncomplaining child sleeping head-up on port tack, feet-up on the starboard!

Sailing-club dances were the other large part of the nautical social scene. In an era when sports grants and related handouts did not exist, the annual club dinner-dance was essentially a fundraiser, well supported and much enjoyed for the good meals on offer at the Butler Arms hotel in Waterville, and for the Big Band dance music that went on until the early hours of the morning.

Pat and our cocker spaniel, Nero, sailing in the 1960s.

That was later days. One month prior to our first wedding anniversary saw us bereaved and dazed by the loss of a full-term baby daughter. On 11 August each year, I still flail around in my head, looking for someone or something to blame – the carelessness or incompetence of the doctor, the inadequacy of the hospital maternity services … but the liability always comes back to me. Why did I not shout? Why did I not scream for *someone* to do *something* when Pat's labour went on too long?

May I plead abysmal ignorance? May I plead worldly inexperience? May I plead that I hadn't an earthly clue about the process or complications of childbirth? May I plead also – nay, *state categorically* – that the medical profession of rural Ireland in the 1950s was untouchable, was beyond scrutiny, was beyond adverse comment, and was far, far beyond answerability? Today, some six decades later, I quote from a recent *Irish Times* article (18 November 2019):

> Many bereaved parents were simply advised to go home, get some rest, try to put it behind them (an impossibility), and have another baby – a false and misguided remedy that did not fix their pain but merely served to bury it deeply.

On my eighty-sixth birthday, I learned that a woman who had shared that maternity ward with Pat in 1957 had a successful delivery on that occasion but lost her second baby in the same establishment and under the same care. She did not return there for subsequent births. Neither did we.

And today, the multiple roles of judge, jury, prosecutor and defendant that have been going on in camera in my head for more than six decades have not been resolved. Baby Lisa, had she lived, would be over sixty years of age today, and would have brought us as much joy daily as did Céline, born in 1959, and Linda, born in 1963. Just as they still bring me joy today – Linda in San Francisco, and Céline, with husband Steve Maloney and two sons, Sam and Jackson, in Butte, Montana.

Meanwhile, the daughter we never knew, and the elder sister that Céline and Linda never knew, lies in the grave of her O'Neill great grandparents 'over the water' in Cahersiveen, where undertaker Mick Fitzpatrick and I silently placed her...

The Counsellor

As friends lay bare their souls in verse or prose,
Who knows what pain or joy the lines expose?
But wonder more what other tales concealed
Between the lines can never be revealed.
Out-speak of love, rejection, loss or fear.
I hear. Your Counsellor is near.
Do whisper or scream-out in thunder rolls,
For telling is a therapy for souls.
I envy every potent word that flows.
My inner fears forever must repose,
Barred from the solace of the open air,
While I convince myself they are not there.

7

DIVING DAYS

I t was a strange experience back in the 1950s to see humans in black rubber suits cavorting about in the shallows of Valentia harbour with air tanks and breathing apparatus. These were early days, when the underwater adventures and photography of Jacques Cousteau or of Hans and Lotte Hass in the Mediterranean or the Red Sea had just appeared in popular print. There was no serious diving-equipment supplier nearer to Valentia than Stoke-on-Trent in England, and yet here were these divers, who hailed from Queen's University in Belfast, using air tanks that were recycled from some aircraft equipment, making it look very easy indeed to access the bottom of Valentia harbour.

This first sight of wetsuits and air cylinders was captivating; I was destined for the diving road. This was confirmed for me by a further similar experience in June 1959, when two Dubliners, Tom Shakespeare and Billy Crowley, arrived at Valentia and let me try on one of their neoprene suits and discover for myself for the first time that there *was* a means of swimming in the ten-degree Atlantic Ocean without dying from pneumonia. In any case, I was hooked, and I headed for the water with – figuratively speaking – the 1953 edition of Cousteau's *The Silent World* in one hand and a prayer book in the other! Indeed, Pat may also have offered a few initial, silent prayers as I ventured into the deep; nonetheless, she was totally supportive of my extreme scheme.

Bord Fáilte was not interested in our proposal to set up a diving centre. Diving, indeed! In Ireland's freezing waters? The august Tourism Board refused to touch it with a pole, preferring to flog existing horses, however dead. 'New products' and 'potential' were not yet the buzzwords of Baggot Street Bridge.

Like 'The Cable' of the distant 1860s, the activity of scuba diving in the equally unenlightened 1960s was regarded as bordering on black magic. Even if we had no support, neither had we any competition. It would be ten years before our new diving-holiday service had any imitators anywhere in the country, and a further twenty years would pass before every pier-head and every street corner in the country would have its ubiquitous dive shop.

Spearfishing was in vogue then. I had already visited the underwater sands of Glanleam and Beginish beaches with snorkel, face-mask, bare skin and a brush-handle spear to fetch many a plaice or flounder for the table, but the Irish Open Spearfishing Championship of the era brought competitors, visitors and income to an island that was in the throes of a downhill slope. The *Curragh Sub Aqua Club Diving News* of Autumn 1964 gives an insight into the activity and highlights generated by the Irish Open Spearfishing Championship of that year:

> Sunshine, fine weather, fifty-six competitors, including teams from Liverpool, Scarborough and Bridlington, Yorkshire ... The attendance of the Valentia Pipe Band at the fin-off and weigh-in ... Multicoloured tents with the respective club banners on the seafront campsite ... Winning team: Curragh Sub Aqua club – John Hailes, Mick Moriarty, Bernie Brennan, Tommy Coyle ... Winning local boatman, Dom Burke ... Prizes presented at the Gala Diving Dance in the island's hall....

With Mom and Dad, ready for Sunday Mass.

A good bamboo for sailing
a tin-can-made boat.

A trike for Christmas!

Christmas also meant books for me. Some of
these, bearing inscriptions in Dad's hand, are
treasured family artefacts in San Francisco and
Butte, Montana.

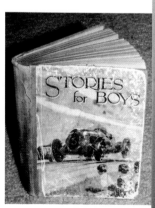

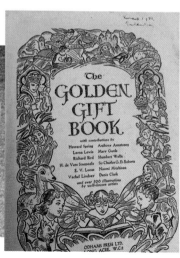

Roller skates at last!

Together again, Jim and Eileen Lavelle
on Aranmore Island in 1952, while Jim
was Principal Keeper there.

My 'Inter Cert' of 1949 was
a failure of some distinction.

Pat and I married in Cork on
8 September 1956.

Here, in the extremities of coastal Kerry, stood an industry of worldwide importance, linking the telegraph outlets of Europe with their counterparts in Canada and the United States. Such telegraph artefacts are now on display at Valentia Island Heritage Centre.

Early days in the diving business, with Pat Curtin, Raphael Greene and Mickey 'Dore' O'Connell.

Below left: My 'small ad' in Triton magazine brought us our first international tourists, Irene and Ray Rogers of Liverpool.

Below right: An advertising sticker designed by our Dutch diving friend, Hes.

Spear-fishing champions, 1964, at Valentia. Curragh Sub Aqua Club. (L to R) John Hailes, Mick Moriarty, Bernie Brennan and Tommy Coyle, with boatman Dominic Gallagher.

Below left: Cylinder-filling station in the 1980s.

Below right: A sticker board of diving clubs is a reminder of many international visitors.

So Far and Yet So Near
1963

Above left: The hazards of pram-pushing in the pre-bridge 1960s – Pat and baby Céline on Bachelor's Walk, Valentia.

Above right: 'Warner' aided our bridge cause. His cartoons went far and wide on calendars of the 1960s.

Below: 'Our bridge to everywhere' – Valentia Bridge today.

Above left: Our European advertising initiative brought Pat and myself to Holland where I saw how the Dutch fishermen of Zierikzee had their mussel-dredging rigging down to a fine art.

Above right: Scalloping gear on the *Béal Bocht* following our visit to Zierikzee.

Below: Lemon Rock, County Kerry – a 'stand-in' for Rockall in the 1990s BBC TV series, *The Ambassador*.

Skellig – Island Outpost of Europe was launched at the Listowel Writers' Week in June 1976. (L to R) Paul Robinson, Dominic Burke, Noel Power, Paddy Gallagher, unknown, John B. Keane, John Keane, Marie Coffey, Des.

Below left: Boats of the 1973 season at Skellig.

Below right: Remains of a building on Small Skellig, noted and photographed by me in the 1980s.

American movie star Hugh O'Brian visited Valentia in the 1960s. He is pictured here with myself, Pat and Céline.

That was the exciting, novel sentiment of the time, and so it would continue for several years, until I – among many, many others – would abandon the 'sport' of spearfishing in favour of conservation.

Meanwhile, for me, in 1967 – with my new, Ballybunion-built, 26ft boat, *Sardana* – there was the thrill of providing a new speciality. The pure adventure of diving where nobody had ever dived before brought visitors from far afield. Movie star of the era, Hugh O'Brian, even found us in those earliest of years.

Never a dive-school, we found our target market in the experienced divers of the UK and Ireland – many already tiring of the well-established dive centres of the UK and the long-established centres of the Mediterranean and the Red Sea. The freedom for experienced divers to enjoy a holiday without the responsibility of attending to club trainees was something new, too.

That our initial advert was aimed at a UK magazine was a measure of our novice marketing status. The concept of attracting mainland Europeans to our cold, wild, North Atlantic waters was – like Bord Fáilte's opinion – a bridge too far in those early days.

The novelty of all this and the pleasure of sharing our seas with appreciative visitors locked those initial days into my head – so much so that it is easy to remember that the *Sardana's* first international scuba-diving tourists were Irene and Ray Rogers of Liverpool, who had been influenced to venture to Ireland in 1967 in response to that 'small ad' of 1966 – a very small, two-inch, single-column advertisement that I had placed in two diving magazines of the time – *Underwater World* and *Triton,* the journal of the British

Irene Rogers boarding the *Sardana* at Skellig in 1967.

Sub-Aqua Club. This miniscule advertising initiative and its immediate success must rate it as the best advertising campaign in history because these clients returned the next year and the next and the next.

Diving also offered commercial applications in another direction – the prospect of selectively catching shellfish such as scallops without wreaking havoc on the seabed with steel dredges, or the opportunity of taking crawfish or lobsters without the day-long labours of shooting and hauling pots. Before very long, I had three English divers working for me, and I enjoyed every prospect of making a very efficient business of it. However, one young, self-serving Minister for Fisheries, later to become an old, self-serving Taoiseach, was able to count votes. I was one diving boatman; non-diving, 'traditional' fishermen were legion. Haughey's Bye-Law No. 533 of 1966 put a stop to my diving for shellfish.

Following that hefty blow, it might have been pardonable to hang my head, diminish my horizons and sign on for long-term dole. Instead, in Hilser's jewellery shop in Tralee, I bought a 'silver' cup, named it the '533/1966 Trophy' and presented it for the Valentia National School's annual tug-o-war. In a similar frame of mind, I pursued an earlier order for a new boat – a 32-footer to be built by the BIM boatyard in Dingle, to be delivered by July 1968, and to be named the *Béal Bocht!*

Sadly, as the 1970s hove into sight, the Northern 'Troubles' and the burning of an English tour bus at Renard Point near Cahersiveen on 7 June 1970 put a stop to the emerging UK market of our tourism and diving venture.

I almost left Valentia again then – this time for Tralee. What little residue of book Irish I had retained from my 318/600 result in the 'Inter' exam of 1949 offered me the opportunity to work with Tralee's freelance film cameraman, Pádraig Kennelly, in presenting TV news items 'as Gaeilge' for a fledgling RTÉ.

Being unencumbered with regular employment, I was free to cover every conceivable dogfight – and other equally world-shattering events – from the waves of West Kerry to the coombes of Coolea. We even covered such genuine news items as the first National Farmers' Association protest, when farmers assembled in Bantry, with leader Rickard Deasy, for their memorable, 210-mile Protest March on Dublin, on 19 October 1966.

Kennelly's ingenuity and diplomacy, and his eye for a good photograph, impressed me from that day onwards. The angle of the sunlight was not to his liking, so he turned the whole March-on-Dublin crowd around, making them march in the opposite direction to get the lighting at a better angle – no mean achievement when dealing with an assembly of angry farmers! Eventually, the viewing public would never know that the scenes of marching farmers they saw on TV were headed not for a stand-off in Dáil Éireann, but for the waters of Bantry Bay.

Jacqueline Kennedy also came into our sights and extended our territorial range as far as the Curragh Racecourse on 1 July 1967. I looked forward to this outing as a good opportunity to mix work and Irish Derby pleasure, but Kennelly parked a tripod and camera in front of the stand and gave me orders to keep it trained on Jackie who was in the presidential box with Máirín and Taoiseach Jack Lynch, and to squeeze the trigger if she as much as sneezed. Consequently, with my back to the horses and my eyes glued on the stand, I never saw Lester Piggott win the Derby on *Ribocco*. And unfortunately, Jackie Kennedy did not even sneeze – 'as Gaeilge' or otherwise.

Diving filled the winters of 1966–68. Strangely, the purple sea urchin, *Paracentrotus lividus,* although it might possibly be regarded as 'shellfish' in the loose wording of Haughey's Bye-Law, was not nearly so politically sensitive as were the lobsters, crawfish and scallops that were the law's main focus. Perhaps this had to do with the fact that plentiful urchins were not to be found locally or anywhere near the Iveragh Peninsula other than Kenmare

Bay or Bantry Bay. Nor was there any efficient way other than diving to harvest the vast quantities of urchins that coated the rocky seabed beyond the tidal zone on that coast. It was winter-season activity; it was tough; it was cold. And it left many an irritating urchin spine embedded in knees, knuckles and elbows. But it was work, not alone for me and for fellow-diver Raphael Greene, but for the colourful local Kenmare crew – Nealie-the-Master, Johnny-Bob and Prince – who provided the cover-boat and packed and shipped the expensive delicacies to the ready markets in Paris and Brussels.

Soon, however, there came a new, timely stroke of good luck. Out of the blue, in 1970, two visiting holiday-divers came from mainland Europe. Jos Audenaerd from Belgium and Hes Van Schoonhoven from Holland would ultimately spread our news far and wide in the sports-diving circles of their homelands. It was timely, indeed, as the English tourism market that had been our initial support was now so totally alienated by the Irish political situation that we even discontinued our advertising there and turned our efforts to building up a rapport with mainland Europe. Irene and Ray, our original, stalwart, annual UK visitors, moved to work in Hong Kong in 1975, but other personal friends from Britain would still come, and still enjoy peaceful visits locally – even if long-standing English clients, such as Clive Sheldon, Rick Hazelgrove and Bob Bourne, might well have feared otherwise during a dive at the Valentia Bridge on 4 October 1988, when they discovered ammunition and a discarded .22 rifle barrel.

Our European advertising initiative was a personal, humble effort, aimed largely at the Netherlands and Belgium, where Pat and I would visit dive clubs, while our two new friends, Jos and Hes, gave slide presentations of their holiday experiences in Valentia. A local Belgian or Dutch travel agency might attend; a ferry company might supply some brochures; Aer Lingus was particularly supportive and would send a representative – and often provide a side of Irish smoked salmon or a bottle of Irish whiskey for the event.

Particularly useless, uncooperative, and dismissive, even to the extent of failing to acknowledge successive invitations, was the Bord Fáilte office in Brussels, who never attended anything; any clients we won from those countries were not the fruits of the celebrated Irish Tourism Board.

Linda's studies at the Shannon College of Hotel Management – and eventual practical, related pursuits in Plymouth – saw Pat and myself visiting, and learning from the British Sub-Aqua Club's Plymouth diving centre at Fort Bovisand. Linda's subsequent studies in Switzerland also extended our European horizons – to note the functional efficiency of the Swiss tourist industry on lake and mountain.

Looking back at our old brochures for the early days – foolscap pages cranked out by hand with the kind co-operation of Tom Shortt of the Cahersiveen FCA HQ – I feel that, as a marketing decision, 'the price was right' for the era: our Bed & Breakfast was on offer at £1.50; a packed lunch was 50p; and an evening dinner cost £1.25. Or you could have all of the above, plus a week's dive-boat trips, for £18. There were no complaints about the service anyway. New clients soon became old friends, and word-of-mouth was an economical advertising medium. And it all took place without any great Business Plans, Market Research or Cash Flow Projections. It just worked!

It also worked as a splendid family experience for us. Our early advertising visits to the Netherlands and Belgium took us and our two girls to sights that otherwise we would never have seen. We saw the great ports of Rotterdam, Antwerp and Ostend; we saw the harbour of Scheveningen and its powerful marine radio station that could be heard at sea on Valentia lifeboat off the Kerry coast; we stepped on the decks of the *Bernard Van Leer* – Scheveningen's equivalent rescue vessel; we walked and drove on the old dams and dykes, we saw the new Dutch Delta Works development, where giant, pre-cast concrete caissons, together with rock and stone imported

A 1986 visit to the Netherlands gave us the opportunity to witness master-shipbuilder, Willem Vos, laying down the keel and giant oak frames of the *Batavia*.

from Norway, were finally keeping the North Sea at bay; we admired the canals of Amsterdam and their interlinked routes of international cargo barge traffic; we studied the mussel fishers of the Oosterschelde and the Ijsselmeer; we toured the shipyard site in Lelystad, where, in 1986, master-shipbuilder, Willem Vos, was laying down the keel and giant oak frames for the 56-metre *Batavia*, a replica of the Dutch East-Indiaman sailing ship of 1628 that, in 1999, would rewrite history and sail successfully to Australia, where the original vessel had perished through mutiny and shipwreck.

And in Den Haag, while our friend, Frans Kok, was doing some electrical installations in the Ridderzaal, I could sit and rest a while on the throne of Queen Beatrix!

Meanwhile, on the coast of Ireland in those 1970s and 1980s, commercial divers were few indeed, particularly divers with the mobility of scuba equipment rather than the cumbersome 'hard hat' gear of old, and I

During the 1970s and 1980s, my services as a commercial diver were in demand. I'm pictured here doing a diving job for a Spanish trawler at Valentia in the 1960s.

found my services in demand in harbours from Valentia to Castletownbere to Bantry to Crookhaven to Foynes, and even to Blacksod Bay, where the growing fleets of Spain and France were accustomed to dock and seek shelter or services.

Language barriers posed some initial difficulty. The local 'Tech' in Cahersiveen offered little by way of adult education in that line, and the occasional instructor visiting our island outpost could – rather like Henry Ford – offer any course you wanted so long as it was Woodwork or Home Baking! The remedy was clear: I embraced a Linguaphone course to add some quality and fluency to the harbourside language lessons of earlier days. Spanish came easily – perhaps it had something to do with the 303/400 I had garnered in Latin in that infamous 'Inter' exam of 1949. Very soon, I similarly immersed myself in self-taught French. It was satisfying to consider myself the only man in the country who could remove all sorts of fishing gear, cables, nets and ropes from trawlers' propellers in four languages! Clearly, too, the financial incentive was a better educational carrot than the hazel rod of Knightstown National School or the bamboo canes of St Brendan's Seminary. Besides, the vocabulary of technical marine topics was considerably more interesting to me than 'The girls decorate the temple with flowers' in Latin, or 'The officer is in the house' in Classical Greek.

And if our diving services kept our summers totally engaged in those 1970s, 1980s, and early 1990s, our winter workload was an equally end-less programme of improvements to our guest bedrooms – now numbering eight, since we had managed to buy our rental home, No. 15, and also buy the 'house next door', No. 16, quite readily. Pretty curtains and linens that

Throughout the 1970s, 1980s and 1990s, our diving-fishing-boating efforts kept us busy indeed.

DES LAVELLE
Author of 'Skellig: Island outpost of Europe'.
OPERATES BOAT TRIPS TO SKELLIG
Phone: Valentia 24

Pat had found on our foreign travels – items that had not yet reached Irish stores – fitted the style of the old Victorian architecture rather well.

Equally, those now-distant springtime days that pre-dated fax, mobile phone and internet, created a rewarding, if binding, workload of client-related postal correspondence, queries, reservations and ferry booking that stretched our two-person energies to the limit. In fact, it was a three-person effort because our good friend, Mrs Mary O'Reilly, spent much of wintertime collecting our postal inquiries in Valentia and forwarding them to us for attention while we spent winter months in America on babysitting duties for Céline and Steve who were mature students at the University of Montana, Missoula, when baby Sam Maloney arrived on the scene in 1996.

Eventually – by which time we had already reached a reasonable state

In 1996, it was time to move into our new bungalow in Glanleam (lower right).

of self-sufficiency – a welcome change of policy saw Bord Fáilte coming onside with marketing assistance, and, more importantly, an eventual change of personnel there brought us a precious friend.

It coincided also with a change of policy in our own lives: a realisation that it was time to quit our intensive diving days, time to sell our oversize home, time to move into our long-awaiting new bungalow in Glanleam, time to retain our venerable *Béal Bocht*, and time to limit our energies to just one principal, growing marine activity – passenger-boat services to the Skellig Islands…

8

A BRIDGE TO
EVERYWHERE

I n the 1950s, we were full of great 'do-good' ideas for changing the world. Muintir na Tíre, a rural, community self-help organisation, was newly in the air, and we embraced it expectantly. I even found myself elected Honorary Secretary, and fully supplied with headed, carbon-copy notepaper pads for petitioning various authorities for sundry local benefits. There was only one catch. The more radical ideas that we, the outnumbered younger members of the Committee, espoused were invariably amended or voted down by the seniors who were quite content to rest on the old glories – political and economic – that Valentia had enjoyed for several generations when the island was the centre of the world in matters of international communications. Equally, and rightly, Valentia regarded itself as the centre of South Kerry in matters of local agricultural prowess. In a 1950s nutshell, Valentia's way of life provided reasonable financial comfort for some, and an understandable, consequent unwillingness to rock the political boat that was sailing rather well in their direction.

In fact, the boat that we younger people viewed was not sailing at all. Old glories notwithstanding, the vessel was stalled, becalmed, aground, and broken-down. Ever since the mid-1950s and the arrival on the roads of

South Kerry of the family motorcar and the ubiquitous Ford pickup truck, mainland villages of no particular merit were suddenly becoming part of the big wide world, while Valentia was still an island stuck in the middle of the Atlantic Ocean – and going nowhere.

Old guard or new guard, Muintir na Tíre –Valentia style – never achieved very much of world-shattering import; there was not much that was achievable within the financial constraints of the then public purse. Perhaps we got some potholes filled – and there were many indeed that needed it. Pushing out a child's pram was a hazardous expedition, and but for the fact that the pram wheels of the 1960s were about fourteen inches in diameter, the vehicle and its precious contents could readily capsize as it sank axel-deep into the craters. Indeed, a good cameo of the dearth of public services on Valentia is the enduring quotation of one busy housewife that dates from 1957 when ESB canvassers were coursing the island to find out how many households would connect to the new service:

'Missus, will you take the electric light?'

'I'll take the light – but I'd prefer the water.'

In fact, the magnitude of local problems depended on the proximity of the beholder, the endurance of the sufferer and the obduracy of the relevant Authority. As late as 1969, the children of Knightstown National School still endured the same cesspool toilet facility where Paddy Reidy had disposed of Johnny Mawe's hazel cane a full generation previously. Rectifying this glaring inadequacy and introducing flush toilets to the school was surely a worthwhile cause for a local committee?

'No', said the Authority – which in this case was Dr Eamonn Casey, Bishop of Kerry. His obdurate resistance to our project was quite beyond our comprehension, but in a measure of the mettle that was arising in Valentia, we took him on verbally, and won the day at a memorable meeting in Chapeltown National School – even if I had to put my money where my mouth was and thump a personal £50 cheque as a deposit on the table before him.

But such community achievements, great or small, hardly mattered in the greater scheme of things. In that era, there was only one major project, one major committee, one major goal that superseded all else – the long-sought-after Valentia Island Bridge.

As far back as 1906, Valentia Islanders were sick of being islanders. That was the year when a campaign began for some connection with the mainland – *any* connection that would be an improvement on the available ferries. Committees sat, as they always do; petitions were sent, as they always are; matters were given consideration, much of it. And eventually World War I put an end to all that. Peacetime came again – to the world, if not to the Valentia Bridge question – and more committees sat, and more petitions were sent, and they were considered again. And World War II put an end to that.

But 1948 eventually came. A new government was perceived to be more amenable to the bridge concept and, coincidentally, a particular Cahersiveen 'Fair Day' with very bad weather and exceptional difficulties for island farmers and their animals on the ferry brought matters to a head once more. At last, the committees were no longer sitting and discussing. Under the leadership of Con Lyne of Ballyhearney, they were standing up and taking the fight to the Authority's door.

On 23 June 1949, the first Valentia Bridge deputation headed to the County Hall in Tralee, and on 20 June 1951, Valentia Bridge finally got a mention in Dáil Questions when Jack Flynn, TD asked the Minister for Local Government (Mr Smith) if he would 'provide the necessary money for the erection of a bridge from the island to the mainland at the earliest possible date'.

Nobody in charge of public money – central government or county council – really wanted to spend it on a bridge to Valentia, and the Minister's reply reflected this: 'In view of the present position and the commitment of the Road Fund, it is not possible to allocate any grant towards the erection of this bridge.'

The County Council members were no more forthcoming. Councillor Charlie Lenihan, in a 'To Hell or to Connacht' attitude, even suggested that it would be cheaper to move all 971 souls out of Valentia and house them somewhere in the midlands! The more calculating public representatives, when finally forced into a corner by the findings of a Public Inquiry in 1955, resorted to procrastination as a tool. Yes, a bridge could be sanctioned; *but* plans would take time and surveys would take time and there would have to be a competition for designs and that would take time and, when the main plans were received, there would also have to be an opening span, and that design would take more time…

However, Valentia had no stomach for any more time. The clock had been ticking for fifty years, and that was long enough. Islanders were still frequently marooned on one side or the other when the lash of south-easterly gales, coupled with spring tides, rendered Knightstown piers untenable – even forcing the ferry boats to abandon the island completely and seek shelter in Cahersiveen. Island farmers still took poorer prices at the Cahersiveen fairs because of the difficulty of getting animals to market, or the prospect of taking them home unsold and facing the same hardship twice. The closure in January 1960 of the Farranfore–Renard rail-link that had served the South Kerry outposts since July 1893 further exacerbated Valentia's isolation.

Medical emergencies added fuel and credibility to the islanders' predicament. On 26 February 1961, when a south-west gale closed all normal ferry communications, the Valentia lifeboat had to be called in to bring the County Surgeon and his assistant to the island to perform an emergency operation. An equivalent crisis occurred at 1.15am on 12 May 1964, when even the lifeboat had great difficulty in evacuating a female patient from the island in a dreadful storm. The County Council, though, was not impressed by such urgencies, and official delaying tactics continued. When the long-mentioned site-survey finally came round, official procrastinators insisted that not only was the narrowest span to be surveyed, but also the widest and the deepest.

Nonetheless, Valentia pressure continued relentlessly. Activists of the island's senior and junior wings, now tightly united, and with the invaluable assistance of sympathetic newsman Pádraig Kennelly of Tralee, sallied forth in monthly deputations to County Council, to government ministers, to consultant engineers, to photographers, journalists, and public relations experts. Cartoonist 'Warner' joined our battle, and his satirical cartoons on officialdom's inactivity went far and wide as topical calendar illustrations of 1963 and 1964. Still no bridge, still no final design, still no opening-span decisions, but, as one observer noted, 'Enough documentation, reports and files to dump in the harbour and make an adequate causeway to the island!'

Finally, Fate took a fortunate hand. Mrs Crowley, TD for South Kerry, passed away in 1966, and her passing did more for the Valentia Bridge project than every delegation, every county councillor and every government minister combined. The Government of the time was left in dire need of retaining Mrs Crowley's Fianna Fáil seat while facing a considerable challenge from Fine Gael's Michael Begley.

John O'Leary of Killarney was the Fianna Fáil candidate; Neil Blaney, TD, was the party's Director of Elections. A deal was struck – helped in no small way by the rousing, Kilcormack-style, pulpit language of the island's parish priest, Fr Beasley, who was even prepared to mount Blaney's political platform for the cause – and if Valentia voted Fianna Fáil, we *would* get our bridge.

We did just that. In the by-election of 4 December 1966, John O'Leary of Fianna Fáil won the seat by a slender 783-vote majority. The *Kerryman* newspaper of the following weekend summed it up: 'Valentia, with the promise of a bridge, voted heavily for O'Leary.' We were not bashful about trumpeting Valentia's contribution to the result and could justifiably boast: 'We delivered. Now it's your turn!' Our newfound political ally, Neil Blaney, Director of Elections and Minister for Agriculture and Fisheries, kept his word too.

Things began to move. Perhaps they were moving too fast for some of the county councillors who were accustomed to chewing on this old tobacco year after year. At the Council meeting of 20 February 1967, some of the members did not even know which of the competing contractors they had already chosen; some thought that the winner was John Paul & Co., whereas in reality, it was P.J. Hegarty & Sons Ltd.

'Work on Valentia Bridge in two months,' headlined the *Kerryman* on 11 March 1967, with the details that ministerial sanction had been received for P.J. Hegarty's tender of £365,910. But 'Who'll Foot the Bill for Valentia Bridge?' was a bigger headline in the following issue, as the councillors – some still smarting from the recent election, others still elated by it – argued and sniped amongst themselves about the value of the central government grant and the fact that interim 'add-ons' had brought the overall cost of the bridge to £410,000. Should they accept a 50 per cent central grant or hold out for 75 per cent? It was all about playing for time. But time finally ran out for them. Work on the Valentia Bridge began in September 1967.

The shovel and related tools had been anathema to me since childhood days when I had been obliged to 'weed and earth the spuds' at moments when I would have preferred to be sailing periwinkle boats on the beach with my colleagues. Nonetheless, when the long-mythical Valentia Bridge project finally materialised, I pocketed the delusions of grandeur that my recent Cable Station job had nurtured for sixteen years and three days, and I joined the labour force of bridge contractor P.J. Hegarty & Sons.

Accessing Portmagee was no easy matter for a Knightstown dweller in those days; there was a long, watery channel in the way. But John (Francis) Curran, also a Cable Station 'leftover' like myself, joined the bridge workforce too, and via ferry – or via my Knightstown-based punt and my Renard-based car – we commuted daily to Portmagee.

Jerry O'Mahony was a foreman of some perception. He either noted my inadequacy as a budding labourer or became aware of my more useful mechanical and electrical skills that came from my Cable Station years. Either way, I found myself running and maintaining the generator that was the heart of the project's pile-driving operations, or occasionally ensconced indoors on wiring and electrical jobs around the site offices.

However, I did not persevere very long. A much more interesting alternative was at hand: my new boat, the 32ft *Béal Bocht*, built of oak and larch by foreman John Reagan of Dingle's BIM yard, was delivered in July 1968, replacing my original *Sardana* of 1967. I was on my way to being a full-time fisherman. Or so it seemed at the time…

I did not know then how many days, weeks or years of my life I would spend trying to explain the complexity of the name *Béal Bocht* to uncomprehending foreign visitors! Indeed, in desperation, to anyone who had any spark of understanding, I often stated that if I ever got another boat, I would name her the *Béal Dúnta*! Frequently, of course, this would serve only to extend further the questions and explanations. And my promise of owning a *Béal Dúnta* – a 15ft glass-fibre punt – would not come true until some forty-seven years later.

Meanwhile, in 1967, P.J. Hegarty & Sons managed to carry on quite well in my absence, and the bridge's final beams and decking slipped into place at the end of November 1969, linking island and mainland. The fact that it still lacked a few bells and whistles did not alter the concrete fact that the connection was made.

However, officialdom still regarded it as a building-site and maintained a padlocked gate at either end. Valentia was still an island! Of course, these barricades were something that could be circumvented at a late hour if you knew the watchman. Similarly, the barricades could be breached in the dead of night if, like many Valentia car-owners, you kept a bolt-cutter in the toolkit.

But these were hardly satisfactory measures, and eventually the cloak-and-dagger crossings and the protracted 'building-site' regulations began to wear a bit thin with Valentia Islanders. Musketeer John Condon of my early days now came back into our lives and into our cause in his chosen field of TV production, carrying our arguments and our impatience nationwide on his *Newsbeat* programme. Hegarty's spokesman tried to make capital with the argument that even though the bridge was strictly a building site, the local ambulance was allowed to cross for emergencies. On screen, I scorned this sop with the rebuttal, still on film in the archives of RTÉ, 'You would do as much for a sick dog!'

Blood was up. Fight was in the air. Echoes of the Parisian student riots of May 1968, when disgruntled, impatient students and workers brought 800,000 protestors onto the streets, were still on our minds. Valentia citizens, disgruntled and impatient too, could do no less. And so, on a fine day in May 1970, we set out *en masse* to storm the Valentia Bridge barricades!

If there had been a few disbelievers throughout the long years of the bridge campaign, or if there had been a few who might have been happy if it never reached fruition, there were no such reservations now. The most united moment of Valentia's long history climaxed as islanders young and old descended on the Valentia end of the bridge site – on foot, on bikes, on tractors and trailers and horse-drawn vehicles. Padlocks, barbed wire and verbal warnings turned to water before the onslaught. Donal Burns was the first over the barricade; I was second; and all of Valentia followed. Elderly ladies who could not surmount the defences forced their way through apertures where a snipe couldn't fly; babes in arms were passed through gaps where a wren couldn't perch; and all of Valentia's citizens proudly marched to the Portmagee site offices of P.J. Hegarty & Sons, made known their annoyance about the unacceptable delays, and made an orderly return home by the same route.

P.J. Hegarty & Sons eventually capitulated; the bridge, still short of its bells and whistles, saw traffic flowing on 1 October 1970. It was not 'official', but at that stage we had endured our fill of officialdom, and rather than wait for the County Council and the various related interests to proceed at their chosen pace, Valentia decided to have its own 'official' opening.

And a Grand Opening it was – on 1 January 1971 – with wind and rain doing little to dampen the enthusiasm. And even if the officiating attendees

With wind and rain doing little to dampen the enthusiasm, the unofficial Grand Opening of the Valentia Bridge finally took place.

– Dr Eamonn Casey, Bishop of Kerry, and Church of Ireland Minister, Rev. Canon Enright – were blissfully unaware of the fact that the event was not quite the 'official' function, it did not detract from the fullness of their official blessing.

But the bridge would not be without its problems. Electrical/mechanical/hydraulic unreliability would soon be of concern – particularly in relation to lifeboat services to any incident south of Valentia. Half an hour could be saved by taking the short-cut through Valentia harbour and the Portmagee channel – provided that the bridge could be opened on time. But this was not always the case, and it forced us to keep a clearly painted line of a certain high-water mark on the wall of the Valentia dock. If the line was visible, the lifeboat of the time, the *Rowland Watts*, could get under the bridge;

A timely cartoon by 'JOD' – and an appropriate dedication by Neil Blaney for Céline – for our 'unofficial official' Opening Day, 1 January 1971.

" *When I was a girl, Mr. Blaney, you said we'd be the first to cross the Bridge. That's how you got my vote in '66.*"

if the line was underwater, it meant taking the long way round – at the cost of an extra half an hour.

Then came a situation when the bridge opening span became stuck halfway open/closed. Neither vehicle nor vessel could pass, forcing the organisation of a very impromptu ferry to get a wedding party to its appointment on the other side.

Finally – to the great annoyance of visiting yachtsmen – the opening machinery would no longer function, and rather than sail jauntily up or down the length of the Portmagee channel, they too had to take the long way round – and the rougher option to the west.

Today, the bridge is a fixture. Its idle hydraulics and electrics are hanging in rusty shards beneath the deck, and the joints of the 'opening' span – which rattle loudly by day, and even more so by night – are filled with tarmac.

Be that as it may, it is our bridge to everywhere – a concrete monument to a long, hard-won campaign.

9

RYAN'S DAUGHTER

Colonel Bill O'Kelly came to visit me in Valentia in the autumn of 1968. He was the liaison officer of the Faraway Productions Film Company, based in Dingle, and he needed a diver/boatman and general Marine Adviser for the production that would eventually become David Lean's epic of war, betrayal, religion, sex and infidelity – the movie, *Ryan's Daughter.*

Colonel O'Kelly's proposal might be regarded as just a great stroke of luck for this South Kerry boatman, or it could be viewed in light of the fact that my name was already in the public eye as a commercial scuba diver – at a time and a place where such activities were rare indeed. Either way, it did not take much persuasion on his part to convince me that this was an offer I could not refuse. It promised busy days when action was called for, adequate stand-down times to slip home to Valentia occasionally, rewarding work in terms of job satisfaction, as well as remarkably good wages and living expenses on which we could really *live!* Very promptly, I changed my earlier plans of being a full-time Valentia Island fisherman.

Shutting up shop on Valentia and moving with my boat to Dingle for the proposed duration of three months did not sound too difficult a prospect. Soon I was booked into a friendly B&B at Alpine House in Dingle, and the *Béal Bocht,* with Richard Connolly of Valentia as a live-onboard crewman, was standing by at Dingle pier. One of our Dingle friends, Micheál Keane, would later let me park a caravan on his land until Pat and the girls would join me in a rental house after Christmas.

The rental-house project was easier said than done. All habitable buildings – and many that were not – were snapped up by movie-related personnel. House refurbishment – at the expense of Faraway Productions – became a major industry. Crooked rooms were squared, sagging floors were levelled, leaning door-frames were plumbed, bathrooms were added, cookers and furniture were installed. And it was just as well that such home comforts were finally available – my Dingle contract of three months soon became twelve, and a further winter would similarly be spent in Kilkee on the coast of Clare to get the shooting of Atlantic storm scenes on cliff and beach completed. But this was 1968; we were young, my *Béal Bocht* was going well, and we were ready for whatever the movie life might offer.

If I had one qualm, it was the question of taking Céline and Linda out of their familiar Knightstown National School and starting them anew in the town environment of Dingle. But I need not have worried; the kids mastered every back lane and back yard in the vicinity long before I did!

Working in the Special Effects Department, my input entailed setting up marine situations in advance of shooting schedules. It also meant traversing every beach, cliff and crag of the Dingle peninsula, as well as every square mile of the surrounding inshore waters from Minard to Coumeenole to Sybil Point – and later, from Loop Head to the Bridges of Ross to Kilkee.

Rather distinct from the panic and pressure of the typical movie set where everyone invariably wants results 'instantly' or 'now' or 'yesterday', not even David Lean could move the tides, and consequently our marine projects were seldom instant or now or yesterday, as we waited half a day for the tide to come in or half a day for the tide to go out. Add in adverse weather conditions, and it could take a week to complete a simple job of anchoring rafts loaded with guns and ammunition in positions where they could conveniently be 'blown ashore' in 'storm conditions' under the cameras. Inevitably, of course, as soon as everything was in place, the Producers, the Directors, or somebody equally near to God, would rewrite the entire shooting schedule and call for our work to be undone again – until the next time.

Even the birds of the air worked for the movies in Dingle at that time. The shooting of one particular springtime love scene in the woods, between Rose Ryan (Sarah Miles) and Major Randolph Doryan (Christopher Jones), was not going well. In fact, it was going very badly, largely because of a personality clash between the two principals, and the springtime woodland scene soon became a summertime woodland scene – and seemed to be headed for an autumn scene … or worse. But with Lean's typical 'get the shot at all costs' attitude, a dancehall was hired in Murrioch, Ballydavid, and an artificial woodland scene was created indoors. A courier was sent to a London butterfly farm for a box of live butterflies to authenticate the indoor set. Wild birds were trapped locally and released on the set. But still the shot was not working.

Time went on. The butterflies had thrived and were even moving on into old age, and the local birds were being so well fed indoors that they were growing fat in the process. Still there was no success with the love scene. One day, I went into the hall for some piece of electrical equipment – a day when there was no human activity there – and as I opened the hall door, a robin flew out. No problem – there were plenty more inside. But when I opened the door to leave, the robin flew back in. Movie life was the Good Life – even for the birds.

Lean's passion for perfection was evident in even the smallest of scenes – and particularly in one small shot in the middle of the huge scene of music and dance at the wedding night of Charles Shaughnessy and Rosie Ryan. The fiddle player's facial expression was not quite right as he leered and grimaced towards the honeymoon bedroom of the newly married pair. 'Cut! Cut! Cut!' The scene – a tight close-up of the musician's face – was shot again and again while he played his best and leered his best and grimaced his best. But it still was not right – until Assistant Director Pedro Vidal, out of shot, got down on his knees and began groping the fiddler sexually. Only then did the appropriate facial expression materialise, and the shot was promptly 'in the can'!

Leo McKern had a splendid yacht – the 33ft sloop, *Nutkin* – and when he wasn't acting the part of Tom Ryan, father of Rose, and being a toady and an informer and selling out on his countrymen, he too spent much of his time on Dingle Bay, where we in our work and he in his leisure would meet

For some forty years, I kept a supply of high-quality poitín on the *Béal Bocht*, in a little bottle labelled 'Compass Fluid'.

frequently. Leo's ship's stores were much more varied than ours. Among other concoctions, he had a very fine supply of high-quality poitín, which – he claimed – came from the Dingle gardaí. But it was his collateral use of the poitín that impressed me: he kept his yacht's leaking compass topped up with it! I followed this 'First Aid' tip for some forty years on my own *Béal Bocht*. And when anyone disbelieved the story, I would point to a little bottle with a handwritten label, 'Compass Fluid', and say, 'Sniff that!'

My close association with Leo McKern was rather unusual in movie life. Usually, the actors and the technicians had minimal social association. A mutual disrespect for one another was more the order of things. The 'Stars' clearly thought that we, the technicians, would be out of work without their big-name, headline-grabbing input; we, the technicians, *knew* that without our technical know-how, the 'Stars' would stand idle on beach, cliff or set. But it was a mindset that harmed neither party.

The script of *Ryan's Daughter* called for a gunrunning ship – an old, well-worn, workhorse that would fit into the 1916 setting. Of the dozens of trawlers in Dingle at the time, not one of them would fit the bill. But the *Granat*, an ancient Danish-built vessel belonging to Christy O'Shea of Valentia, was just right. She was diesel-powered but the addition of a fake smokestack would promptly turn her into a sleazy, gunrunning steamer. This installation was done in advance, and the deal was made for the *Granat* to show up in Dingle, ready for filming the following week. And she did. But in the interim, Christy had given her a new paint job like never before, and the gleaming ship that arrived in Dingle was not the shabby old tramp steamer that was ordered.

Consternation! Directors foamed at the mouth, schedules were rescheduled, and several camera crews and assorted 'Stars' were stood down while a team of the company's painters descended on the vessel. It took just three hours, and the *Granat* was restored to her shabby, grimy, rusty, battered old self, and thus sailed into the movie world.

Tradesmen of other skills on the film set were equally professional, and could fabricate, fix, or make just about anything to fit a particular occasion. Peter Dukelow's plasterers could – and did – build a totally credible village of glass-fibre façades. Bob MacDonald's metalworkers built everything from wind-machines to wave-machines and needles and anchors. Bernie Prentice's electricians created daylight where there was none. Freddie Young's cameramen made night-time where it was day. And when David Lean found that the summer beaches of the Dingle peninsula in 1969 were not sunny enough, he simply sent a crew to South Africa to get the necessary brief shot of Fr Collins (Trevor Howard) and Michael (John Mills) carrying a naomhóg across the sunny sands.

Eventual filmgoers would never know that this particular naomhóg was not the real thing; it was the brainchild of Bert, the Special Effects Department's carpenter, who carved the full-sized vessel out of a solid block of expanded polystyrene, cut it into four sections, and crated it to South Africa, for convenient reassembly on the new set – Nordhoek beach, a few miles from Cape Town.

Back in the real and stormy world of Coumeenole beach on Slea Head, we could have lost both Trevor Howard and John Mills when their genuine naomhóg overturned in the surf of another scene. Mills being hospitalised in Dingle made the news, but we could just as easily have lost twenty lesser actors and extras in a storm at the Bridges of Ross on the coast of County Clare. And nobody heard about it.

Picture a long, sloping rock formation leading at a gentle angle from grassy fields right down into the Atlantic. Picture a raging sea down at the foot of the slope, making a wild backdrop for a group of villagers – men and women – running right to left across the rocks, intent on salvaging the arms and ammunition boxes that were being washed ashore nearby. Picture the camera located at the top of the slope – well out of reach of the sea and well uphill of the actors' action. The scene – with typical Lean exactitude – was shot half a dozen times, but he still was not satisfied. A tea break was called, and everyone abandoned the rocks and retreated up to the field to join the catering wagon.

It was at this moment that the ocean went mad. A veritable tidal wave swelled up from nowhere, swept up the slope and reached waist-high on the camera tripod. The rocky track where twenty actors had been running just moments previously was suddenly under five metres of raging water that, in receding, took everything in its reach – £10,000 worth of lighting equipment, wardrobe items, film boxes. It could just as easily have taken half the crew!

That was lesson enough for one day; a 'wrap' was called, and we lived to film again. Safety lines were more in use after that, and in one close-up scene where Ryan was wading in the surf, the old-fashioned sisal rope that he used for a security line had a stainless-steel cable woven into its heart.

That near-disaster at the Bridges of Ross led to other effective improvisations: our Special Effects technicians built great towers of scaffolding, and chutes with great tubs of water on top, where a pull of a lever dumped wave after huge wave upon close-ups of actors and stand-ins; the unit's mobile water pumps showered effective torrential rain and spray on unfortunate film extras; and when nature wasn't stormy enough, the Kilkee fire brigade stepped in to layer 'storm-foam' on surrounding rocks and creeks. These chemical suds were equally as effective and much safer than anything the Atlantic could offer.

The final shoot of my movie career never took place at all. This was to be the filming near Loop Head in County Clare of Rose Ryan's parasol being blown over the cliffs – to be recovered from the sea by Michael and Fr Collins in their naomhóg. Following a pleasant, eight-hour cruise from Valentia, my *Béal Bocht* and myself and a part-time crewman, Dan O'Driscoll, arrived in Kilbaha harbour to stand by for the planned action. We stood by; and we stood by; and one postponement after another did not bother us in the least. On board the *Béal Bocht*, we had all the necessities of life – a gas cooker, a kettle and a frying pan – and for life's little luxuries, Keating's friendly pub stood by only 50 yards from the pier.

Not much was happening at Kilbaha pier in that era, and if the rare visitor strolling the quayside raised an occasional eyebrow at our odd cargo of umbrellas and authentic-looking ammunition cases, rifles and dynamite boxes, nobody drew the police upon us. Thus, we enjoyed a very peaceful, pleasant, and idle visit, and were quite disappointed when Faraway Productions cancelled the shoot entirely, thus calling a halt to our splendid West Clare sojourn, and leaving me with a cargo of assorted movie props – including two authentic-looking rifles that are still on exhibition in my home and Céline's some fifty years later!

So, it was 1970. And my eighteen-month affair with *Ryan's Daughter* was over. Emboldened by our experiences, Pat and I took the month

This authentic-looking rifle was part of a cargo of assorted movie props that I was left with when Faraway Productions cancelled a shoot at Loop Head, County Clare.

of September off, kept the girls out of school, and headed on a family camping holiday to Spain.

Valentia, Ireland to Valencia, Spain was the target. The date was important: it was 8 September – our wedding anniversary, and also the birthday of daughter Linda. A gala dinner to suit the occasion was planned for the ferry trip from Rosslare to France. Big spenders, movie style!

Our cabin and the girls' cabin had consecutive numbers, and while this looked fine on the booking slip, cabin 101 was on one side of the ship and 102 was on the other. But I could live with that. The sea conditions were not good either. But I could live with that, too. I was thinking exclusively of the forthcoming celebratory feast to which I was looking forward with relish … until we reached the Tuskar lighthouse. Then things went very wrong: my three would-be dining companions suddenly lost their appetite. No banquet, no celebration. Pat retired to our cabin, the girls to theirs – and I spent my anniversary night lurching across the heaving ship from cabin 101 to cabin 102 as a health-visitor for three seasick passengers, who, when morning came, were happy indeed to land on the *terra firma* of Cherbourg!

We had a brand-new tent for the mission. It had never been taken out of its sack. And, for all my childhood Wild West fantasies, I had never pitched a tent in my life. However, by sneaking surreptitious glances at the confident activities of other campers, we managed to erect an adequate shelter for our first night under canvas, and by the time we reached Spain, we were masters of the camping art … well, almost…

A campsite called La Ballena Alegre, 'The Happy Whale', near Barcelona had a peculiar, vaguely familiar smell, which we failed to identify, but it did not deter us from setting up our tent and organising ourselves for a balmy evening meal al fresco. It was a busy site, but before we were halfway through our meal, we noticed that everyone had disappeared. 'Gone to the shops or to the bar,' we thought, and continued dining…

Then they descended upon us – not the missing campers, but the bugs, millions of them, gathering for their evening meal of fresh, fair-skinned, Irish flesh. Mosquitoes! We shot indoors, but not before we had been savaged from head to toe. Too late also, we recognised the smell: it was DDT that had been sprayed on the campsite and on the nearby swamp in a vain attempt to control the pests. We wore the souvenirs of La Ballena Alegre for months – red, sore and itchy. The Happy Whale, indeed! We certainly were not happy campers. But we made it – from Valentia to Valencia, and back.

And to crown the trip, like the final scene of a happy movie, we could now drive all the way home to Valentia Island across the brand-new Valentia Island Bridge.

Above: Down-time on the *Béal Bocht* – somewhere on the Atlantic Ocean!
Left: *Steal Away* in 2010. Well used until our agility did not match hers!
Below: *Béal Dúnta* in 2017, with homemade lugsail and driftwood spars and mast.

Above left: The barque, *Crompton*, wrecked near Portmagee in 1910.

Above right: June 1985, Valentia Lifeboat, *Rowland Watts*, tows the trawler, *Naomh Cáit*, home to Cahersiveen. The crew shown here are Jack Sugrue, Johnny Shea and John Joe Murphy.

Below left: Reminiscing in 2017 on the 1959 loss of the French trawler, *Marie Brigitte*. Photo: Leo Houlihan.

Below right: Cyclists use the Valentia Ferry, for an annual RNLI fundraiser.

Above left: Building my Glanleam home in the 1980s.

Above right: Landing creek at Inishnabro.

Below: Boatmen Des and Kav and a good paint job in spring 2013.

Above: Pat and Linda at California's Alameda docks for Fleet Weekend.

Left: Pat appraises the sculptures at Stanford, California.

Bottom left: Pat with Canada geese, by the Silver Bow Creek at Butte, Montana.

Above: Irene overviewing the city of Butte, Montana, in 2013.

Left: With Irene at Granite Mountain, Butte, Montana, scene of much loss of life in the early mining days.

Below: Irene on the plains of Montana in 2013, near the site of Custer's Last Stand.

Above: Summer activity at Valentia in 2016. Irene and Linda on the *Béal Dúnta*.

Below: A Beginish cruise on the *Béal Dúnta* for Montana visitors, Steve, Céline, Sam and Jackson.

Above left: Irene and myself and a brief flirtation with bicycles in 2012. The anchor from the *Crompton* is in the background.

Above right: Daughters, Céline and Linda, in November 2019.

Below: Blue skies, calm seas and no wind at Knightstown in 2014.

Above left: Home in the snow, Glanleam, Valentia, March 2018. Above right: The harbour beacon at Glanleam is my nearest neighbour. Left: From my window. Sundown, Valentia harbour, and the distant Blaskets.

10

A BROCHURE, A BOOK AND A BOAT TRIP

L ong before the commencement of my commercial boating activity, my horizons had been vividly coloured by a one-off childhood visit to Skellig in the company of Musketeer Adrian and his father, Freddy Mackey.

Now, with my own boat, *Béal Bocht*, could I make a living in 1968 from such a rare, seasonal pursuit? It would be easier than fishing. It could be much more reliable than waiting for any occasional projects that the ocean might offer – if it could be appropriately marketed.

At this stage, it was not a brand-new idea; I had made a few visits with my earlier boat, the *Sardana*, in 1967. Indeed, even long before that, a boat to the Skelligs was already an occasional possibility – if not for tourism visits, then for some lighthouse-service agenda. Jeremiah O'Connell's *Island Lass* featured there in her time, as did the *Curly Wee* of the Royal Hotel, Tony Walsh's *Hester*, the McCrohans' *St Theresa* and James Lynch's *Maria*. Christy Shea's 50ft trawler, *Ros Airgead,* landed there for one memorable outing of the Cahersiveen badminton club in 1968, and a visit in Christy's earlier boat, the *Lobster*, was well detailed in Richard Hayward's *In the Kingdom of Kerry* in 1947. Other boats from Ballinskelligs and Portmagee also made occasional – if rare – Skellig visits when some occasional discerning visitor or authority might pursue the topic and search out a private service.

A feature in *The Kerry Magazine* of 1854, couched in both encouragement and caution, reported in detail on one such visit '…for the benefit of those who may hereafter feel disposed to go to Skellig':

> It is now nigh upon twenty years since a stout boat and a crew of about twenty persons left Valentia roadstead to achieve the adventure of the Skellig. We were warned against a sail-boat, because the weather which is favourable for landing is not the weather for sailing, and tourists have been known to be forty-eight hours rolling log-like at the mercy of the tide within view of the island, but unable either to land or return for lack of a breath of wind to carry them in either direction. Our expedition was better planned and directed by Robert Fitzgerald, son of the Knight of Kerry [who] trusted the attaining of the island to the stout sinews of eight daring men.

And attain it they did, by 11am, and undertook a major island visit, not only of the monastic site, but also enjoying additional extras that are no longer an option in today's circumstances – a tour of the island's two lighthouses to chat with the lighthouse keepers and an opportunity to admire 'the interior brass-work, reflectors, burners [and] fittings, all as bright and burnished as care can make them'. And if this wasn't enough to satisfy anyone's day-trip expectations, the hazardous climb from the North Station lighthouse to the South Peak summit was also included.

However, as well as their admitted major mistake of forgetting to take enough drinking water for the outing, the visitors erred further by becoming so engrossed in their day-long explorations that they neglected to pay any attention to the developing conditions at sea level:

We now descended, after having made a circuit of the island, to the landing place, where a state of things very different from the [morning's] sleepy, placid aspect of the ocean presented itself to our view. Our boat, which we had left moored in a sort of cavern, was now riding some hundred yards off, held against the swell by the efforts of the four men in charge of her, and our old coxswain shook his head as he pronounced that the tide was running like a mill-race and that we must watch the swell of the sea and tumble in [to the boat] as we could without minding a broken shin.

It proved so indeed. The boat was cautiously backed in, and took us off one by one – the boatmen first, as the four men could scarcely manage the unwieldy vessel. Some of us, for want of knowing the exact time to prepare for a swing, were several times obliged to get the boat to go back with the swell of the sea before we got on board. Others with calmer judgement and a better eye succeeded at the first attempt.

Suffice to say that they got home safely to Valentia – even if by moonlight – where:

> …we found supper and bed, not ungrateful after an exciting day's work, to be noted in our reminisces, and here recorded for the benefit of those who may hereafter feel disposed to go to Skellig.

Even some 134 years later, when my *Béal Bocht* arrived on the local scene in 1968, the fact of life – as previously – was that very few people felt 'disposed to go to Skellig'. Few had heard of the islands; and few indeed knew what they offered. Eventually, I began preparing what might today be dubbed a Marketing Plan – a black-and-white 'hang-up' display card and a similarly simple brochure to sell my Skellig boat-trip services in local hotels – of which there were no more than six in my South Kerry horizons at that time, and rather fewer B&Bs.

The brochure seemed like an interesting writing project as the few paragraphs of Skellig information that existed in popular print media of that time could be contained on one side of an A4 page. But on digging deeper – with the help of Cahersiveen and Kerry County Libraries – the scope of my proposed brochure expanded. Indeed, my research became an obsession as I delved into some forty-five published sources and called on the knowledge and co-operation of no fewer than twenty-four helpful colleagues.

Suffice to say that I soon had a great excess of detail for a brochure – and rather more than enough to fill a modest book. But publication of such a book was never on my mind; nor, indeed, had I any clue as to where I might find such a publisher. This was where good luck came in.

Professor Frank Mitchell, a scholar in many disciplines, was a frequent visitor to Valentia from the 1970s onwards. His quest was ancient sites, standing stones and other indications of early settlement of Valentia. He was also a devoted Skellig enthusiast long before such a pursuit was commonplace. Our meeting was inevitable in that context, and a firm friendship ensued. But Frank also had a dependable friend and helper in his wanderings – one Don Roberts. Don himself was an unusual man in that he ran a bookshop in Kilkenny – whose stock included classical books – in an era when bookshops were few and far between.

Through Frank, Don learned of my 'overgrown brochure' and asked to see it. The next step was the crucial one. Don also knew a budding publisher – Michael O'Brien of Dublin – who, at this juncture, already had a number of publications to his credit, including *Proud Island,* by Peadar O'Donnell, *Me Jewel and Darlin' Dublin,* by Éamonn Mac Thomáis, *Tinkers and Travellers,* by Sharon Gmelch, *The Irish Town – An Approach to Survival,* by Patrick Shaffrey,

Hands Off Dublin, by Deirdre Mary Kelly, *The Liberties of Dublin,* edited by Elgy Gillespie, and *Peadar O'Donnell: Irish Social Rebel,* by Michael McInerney. The O'Brien connection clicked, and *Skellig – Island Outpost of Europe* was launched at the Listowel Writers' Week in June 1976; the entire first print was sold out immediately to the McGill/Queen's University Press in Montreal, Canada.

Reprints followed, new editions followed – including a colour section in June 1993 – eventually leading to a full-colour edition and a total rewrite with much greater content, illustrations and up-to-date details, published by the O'Brien Press, Dublin in the spring of 2019 under the title, *Skellig – Experience the Extraordinary.*

At the launch of the new full-colour edition, *Skellig – Experience the Extraordinary,* in Quirke's newsagent in Cahersiveen, in spring 2019.

Thus – and not forgetting a little book, *Kerry* (O'Brien Press, 1986), that I wrote to accompany the splendid photographs of Richard Haughton – I can take pride in having been a very early entry to the O'Brien Press's current stable of 800 titles, and in the fact that the various editions of *Skellig* are the longest-in-print publication of them all!

The publicity for the early editions of *Skellig* generated an additional awareness of the tender ecosystems there-around, and a modicum of growing reliability within the small boating circle of the early days may have helped to spread the Skellig trip's early promotions, but other events negated that somewhat.

An early operator from another harbour visited his attentions upon the passenger-boat concept, but he drew no bouquets upon the Kerry boating scene – marooning a party on the Great Blasket Island for several days in July 1969, until a passing Shell tanker recognised their frantic signals and alerted Valentia lifeboat for the rescue. It became an event recorded by Éamon de Buitléar – of wildlife film fame – who was one of the Great Blasket refugees, together with ornithologist Oscar Merne, Oscar's wife Margaret, and their four-month-old son, as well as a party of British and Irish bird-men who had just come off Inishtearaght. Typically, though, in his memoir, *A Life in the Wild*, Éamon found some humour in a potentially serious situation: 'Luckily, Oscar's wife was breast-feeding her baby, and he was actually fed better than the rest of us.'

The Archbishop of Cashel and Emly was hardly so amused when the same boat operator left him and a party of thirteen stranded at sea in a fog in the middle of Dingle Bay until 11.10pm on 13 July 1969. And for a curtain-call of a later date, the same operator's vessel managed to sink in Dingle harbour some ten minutes after ferrying a group of boy scouts back from the Great Blasket Island.

These – and other – events inevitably drew the attention of various

authorities down upon passenger boats generally, and sent civil servants shuf-
fling through ancient Acts in search of relevant regulations. They did not
find many. The Merchant Shipping Act of 1894 was in the remit of the
Department of Transport and Power, and the Public Health (Amendment)
Act of 1907 was in the hands of Kerry County Council. Neither body had
total responsibility for seafaring topics, and there were gaps and overlaps in
between. The Office of Public Works, custodian of National Monuments,
in launching a programme of Skellig maintenance in 1975, also began to
exert some authority by limiting the ever-increasing number of boats in the
Skellig passenger service.

A far cry from the rare Skellig trips of the nineteenth century or the
reluctant market of the 1970s, by 1984, some nine boats from various harbours served the growing Skellig tourism traffic – and there was wholesale
illegality. If the garbled old regulations were to be applied, no boat should
carry more than twelve passengers, but on 18 July 1989, for example, among
some nine boats at Skellig, the passenger complements numbered 10, 11, 21,
22, 24, 25, 29, 35 and 39!

Indeed, even a decade later, on 20 August 1991, a raid on the Skellig fleet
at sea by Customs and gardaí in a big, powerful, twin-outboard RIB yielded
another harvest of three miscreants – with respective passenger tallies of
23, 16 and 14 passengers. I did not spot this action until it was nearly over.
Luckily, I had only twelve passengers anyhow.

The Department of the Marine had yet to be born. That would happen
in 1993, and the eventual maritime shake-up would be as necessary as it
was uncomfortable. Marine inspectors descended on the boating scene with
gusto, armed with every deep-sea qualification in the world, experienced
in every aspect of marine engineering, experienced in great tankers and
ocean-going cargo ships – experienced in everything, that is, except the
small boats that then constituted the local Skellig services.

'Buoyancy' was suddenly the buzz word. Many of the Skellig boats – *Béal Bocht* included – were 'open boats' that could readily sink if they became full of water. The new 'buoyancy' regulation called for the vessels to be stuffed with enough buoyant material to counter this possibility. A worthwhile idea indeed, but the buoyancy requirements of the *Béal Bocht* called for the installation of expanded polyethylene slabs – the equivalent of thirty bunk-sized mattresses. This was a serious task! I filled every underfloor compartment and also filled the entire cabin – to the exclusion of bunk space or even a spot to sit down. I barely squeezed the installation to allow the retention of the *Béal Bocht's* marine toilet!

That was 1993, and soon a further edict would declare that – in the presence of rainwater – the hull planks could be subject to rot by having all this material stuffed too close. We were ordered to remove the buoyancy slabs and to seal a section of the fore-cabin totally airtight as an alternative buoyancy aid. Again, I managed to save the toilet compartment!

Some further new regulations of that 1993 'buoyancy' year might also raise an eyebrow today. One item that I had to have on board was a little plastic card – a postcard-sized item – called a Rescue Signal Table. Essentially, it indicated that if I saw someone waving a green flag on a cliff top, I could land my boat there. Indeed!

Furthermore, the obligatory first-aid kit for a local Skellig day-trip could no longer be just a tourniquet, a few sticking plasters, a sea-sickness pill and a bottle of Dettol; it had to be the equivalent of a kit found on the life-raft of a transatlantic voyage – a kit containing, among other things, medication for arresting *post-partum* bleeding!

If our Elementary First-Aid certificates did not exactly educate us on this fine point, various other boat-related courses were available for those who might wish to pursue them. I was greatly interested in such pursuit, so much so that my eventual tally of 'tickets' would earn me valuable 'points' long before such qualifications became mandatory:

1. Restricted Cert. of Competency in Radio-telephony, 05.09.66

2. Cert. of Competency, 2nd Hand Special, 11.03.68

3. Basic Sea Survival Course, 02.03.92

4. Radio Operator's Short-Wave Cert., 29.10.06

5. Elementary First-Aid Cert. (Updated), 08.02.17

6. Commercial Endorsement, Category A, 2nd Hand special, (Updated) 13.02.17

The fact that three generations of my Lavelle ancestors had completed a total of some ninety-eight years of service on thirty-six Irish lighthouses is hardly of benefit to my own CV, but my experience in safely landing passengers on Skellig over some forty summers probably counted for a point or two.

This 1993 wave of official attention also forced me to replace a badly cracked port window in the *Béal Bocht's* wheelhouse. I could have replaced it easily years previously, but I did not. In fact, I had resolutely maintained it in that cracked condition because it provided me – and my guests – with a splendid opening to engender chat and repartee on board.

'What happened to your window?' was the morning's inevitable question.

'It was broken by a Special Branch detective with an Uzi sub-machine gun,' was my honest answer. But it was a long story.

My good friend – and ardent Skellig fan with many visits to his credit – Dermot Kinlen had called me to provide two boats for an extended party. His chosen departure point was to be Renard Point. Together with Diarmy Walsh, in his boat, *Agnes Olibhéar*, I brought the *Béal Bocht* to that pier at the appointed morning time. The date was significant – 10 August 1987. The passenger list was also significant – it included a certain Ambassador.

Security was high. A Garda diver was in attendance at Renard Point to examine the underside of our boat for bombs. Other security personnel mingled throughout the party; one of them, a gentleman, puffing contentedly on a smelly, 'hang-down' pipe clenched tightly in his teeth, and with some bulky hardware under a voluminous brown overcoat, stationed himself firmly in the corner of my wheelhouse.

Having been encouraged to sail to Skellig via the north-of-Valentia route rather than pass under the Valentia Bridge with its further possible bomb risk, we set out in some rain and southerly wind. The operation was going quite well, with the pipe-smoker enveloped in a fog of his own making, and the outing's security and communications personnel reporting progress via their hand-held radios to their shore base at regular intervals – until their batteries went flat, that is…

Consternation reigned for a moment. But rather than risk the major base-camp alert that would ensue from any mysterious, sudden silence on our part, I called home with the *Béal Bocht's* VHF radio to ask Pat to phone the gardaí in Cahersiveen to inform the outing's security centre that all was well on the ocean and that progress was normal.

All was normal indeed, particularly in passing Bray Head and encountering the sea conditions that this route entailed. It was also *abnormal* insofar as I was wrong in my belief that the foul sea conditions at that juncture would drive the pipe-smoking, Uzi-toting, Special Branch man outdoors to review his breakfast. They did not. He lurched masterfully about the wheelhouse with every wave until we hit a good 'comber' north of the Lemon Rock, at which point his hardware swung out of control and inflicted a great, fore-and-aft crack in my special, heavy-duty, port-side window-glass. If it bothered him, he did not say; he just stuck to his post – and puffed his smelly pipe.

We reached the Skelligs in some wind and rain, and our visit was carried out without anyone getting shot, bombed or drowned – although the resident Skellig guide, Bob Harris, had suffered rather a shock earlier in the day to encounter a further armed security detail that had arrived on the island unannounced at some early hour.

However, when it was time to go home, the *Agnes Olibhéar* broke down at the Skellig landing. I took her in tow, but the consequent slow trip home was going to delay us enormously; there was no way we could return via the long outward route. I set sail for Portmagee – notifying the nation's security network via the Lavelle domestic network, as before, and asking them to bring the necessary transport to collect the party at Portmagee rather than Renard Point. It was a simple enough solution to a simple enough situation, but when the fleet of highly identifiable 'unmarked' cars began descending on Portmagee, it caused its own local consternation insofar as some feared it was a raid for illegal fishing gear!

Eventually we reached dry land safely – if wet – and security was finally thrown to the winds. All concerned – that certain Ambassador, learned lawyers, sweet ladies, boatmen, embarrassed communications experts, assorted bodyguards, 'unmarked car' drivers, and one dry Special Branch man, now Uzi-less in his open voluminous overcoat, but still puffing his pipe – took to Shanahan's pub for the type of jolly evening that concludes many exciting Skellig visits.

Be it a measure of the security concerns of the time, or a measure of my being unimpressed by visiting personages, the *Béal Bocht's* log for 10 August 1987 merely says: 'Skellig with Kinlen and big crew. Towed *Agnes Olibhéar* home.'

11

BOAT WORK

Skellig trips may have been the potential cream. But the prospect of making a living in the real world of the 1970s called for something more. Thoughts reverted again to the various options that were originally on my table before I had been swept away by the joys, euphoria, excitement and money of the movie business.

Commercial fishing was still a prospect. So was sea angling. Another option was a full-time dive-boat service for sports-diving groups, or a passenger-boat service to off-lying islands. In fact, any job or challenge that the ocean or the harbour might offer was an option.

I undertook them all. There were twenty-five hours in my day then. I drift-netted at sea for salmon in the darkness of summer nights; took sports divers for local dive-trips on summer mornings; ferried local school children – free – to secondary school in Cahersiveen when a brief bus strike left them isolated from their studies; headed for island-visits or other destinations during midday hours; served more scuba divers in the afternoons; and when the day seemed to be done, I was home at the kitchen sink, helping with the wash-up after the great dinners that Pat, capably assisted by Céline and Linda during school holidays, was serving daily to my boating clients.

Novel activities – marine or domestic – were welcomed at the drop of a hat. Pat and Céline even undertook and managed an International Wine-tasting Event on our tennis court on 30 May 1991, when numerous cases of wine were sent to Valentia by Le Saveur Club of France 'to see how they might travel'!

Laid out on a table that stretched from baseline to baseline, and interspersed with Pat's poached salmon and related minutiae, the best French wines 'travelled' particularly well and disappeared rather readily as the related group of visiting Michelin three-starred chefs – including Pierre Troisgros of Roanne, Paul Bocuse of Lyon, Charles Barrier of Tours, Pierre Laporte of Biarritz, Jean Pierre of L'Auberge de l'Ill, Nick Healy of the Dunderry

An International Winetasting Event took place on our tennis court in 1991, when numerous cases of wine were sent by Le Saveur Club of France 'to see how they might travel'.

Lodge, Navan, and Michael O'Callaghan of Longueville House, Mallow – passed judgement. It was a taste-fest that I almost missed through being at sea, but this Valentia sommelier would later pass favourable and enduring comment on the many bottles that the oenophiles and cognoscenti did not even open on the day!

Such novel events were enjoyed as a welcome break from our demanding routine. Equally so, the fabled, annual garden parties at the Sneem home of friend and Skellig fan, Dermot Kinlen – where good funds were raised for charity in absurd auctions of bric-a-brac. Splendid international dishes prepared on occasion by Dermot's guests from the foreign diplomatic corps were in every way unique. And even if the Chinese wine-of-the-day was 'Great Wall', and left 'some-of-us' with the feeling that *the* Great Wall had fallen upon our heads, as night fell, we still had the energy to join our own tireless visitors in providing a substantial local stimulus in Knightstown's pubs.

And that was only the summer timetable. Autumn included mackerel fishing, winter meant scallop fishing, and if there was any spare time, I was building my dream home on the Glanleam Road in Valentia.

But winter also brought an additional boating hazard. Even in the 'shelter' of the Knightstown 'dock-near-the-clock', a south-easter could hurl enough water over that pier to fill the sheltering boats to a near-sinking state. Almost every Valentia boat that ever sought shelter there eventually got the same south-easter dose. It happened to my *Béal Bocht* on one Christmas morning almost too far back to recall; it happened to Diarmy Walsh's *Agnes Olibhéar*; and it happened to Richard Foran's *Mary Sue*.

Petitions to the County Council and to government departments for a higher protective wall fell on such incurably deaf ears that in 1991, we boatmen – for the safety of life as well as of vessels – were ultimately obliged to take the law into our own hands and build the necessary addition ourselves.

Ten men, 700 concrete blocks, a few loads of sand, and a ton of cement soon completed the job and thus eliminated one hazard that had plagued us for too long. The County Council did not approve of our action, but that mattered not to us.

Earlier, it was the same 'inadequate harbour facilities' that had prompted me to run in a Kerry County Council election, on 18 June 1974. I did not succeed. The election quota was 1,763, and I could have won a seat easily if my extended family and friends had equalled just that. As it happened, they registered only 159 votes. Viewed as a consolation, it is probably a larger circle of genuine personal friends than any politician – or would-be politician – can claim. In any event, local self-help – like creating the Marian shrine in the quarry in 1954, like building the dock-wall breakwater in 1991

In July 1976, with the help of crewman Seán Murphy and visiting Dutch diver Hes, I laid a telephone cable across the harbour bed from Renard to Knightstown.

– was a more productive approach than seeking unattainable political office or mounting fruitless petitions to public coffers that were already empty.

Aside from politics, there were other pursuits at hand in those years. In July 1976, with the help of crewman, Seán Murphy, I laid a telephone cable for Telecom Éireann across the harbour bed from Renard to Knightstown and laid a freshwater pipe under the same salt waters for the Kerry County Council. In 1974, with the help of Pat Curtin – and with rope of some two inches in diameter – I hand-made a safety net the size a tennis court for the helicopter deck of a North Sea oil platform. And in a brief, off-season joust with boatbuilding, I built a speedboat in our front dining room.

Even if the window had to be removed to get the vessel outdoors, it was worth the effort. This home-built *San Feliu* with a 40HP Johnson outboard

With the help of Pat Curtin, I hand-made a landing mat for the North Sea oil platform.

and a pair of water skis added another level to our marine activity, as did a Windsurfer sail-board – the first in Ireland – left behind to me by Dutch friend and diver, Franz Kok, following his minor road traffic accident in the locality.

Ornithological studies of the surrounding islands – the Skelligs, Puffin Island and the Blasket Islands – were increasing in those years, and this opened a new source of activity. Seán Murphy was my able crewman on many such missions, and even did the impossible by landing me and a gannet study team on the sheer Small Skellig during one such bird survey in the 1980s, when I also chanced to discover – and photograph – the remnants of an unrecorded, rectangular stone building there. It is on the south face of the island, a spot not visible from passing boats. I gave a copy of this image to an OPW officer of the time, and so was rather intrigued by a headline in *The Kerryman* of 1 July 2020, mentioning the 'discovery' of an 'Early Christian Oratory' on Small Skellig. I offered to share photographs but received no reply. My offer is still open.

An interesting experience of the 1990s was an invitation to visit local schools – Valentia, Ballinskelligs, The Glen, Caherdaniel, Kileenliath, and Waterville – to make 'Skellig' presentations as part of local history lessons. The outings were quite an education for me, too, as I answered a wide variety of questions posed by the children, on topics ranging from archaeology to basking sharks to lighthouses to passenger insurance to wondering if you could keep sheep on Skellig Michael.

Occasional boat services for film crews and advertising companies provided novel impressions. Skellig Michael was invariably the target for all archaeological and wildlife topics, and filming operations were generally rather predictable, but one film-shoot on Puffin Island provided a change. This was a promotion for Weetabix cereal, and the theme was that a dad and a son were on an island walking tour and had brought a pack of Weetabix with them for lunch.

It was a very calm day, so the landing was easy. As soon as the *Béal Bocht* was secured snugly with four-point lines in the Puffin's pier-less, rocky cove, I was happy to give the crew a hand getting the equipment – and numerous cartons of Weetabix – safely ashore and up the steep rocky scree to relatively robust ground. Then I parked myself out of camera to watch the proceedings.

Filming scenic shots to establish the location took quite a while as dad and son scrambled towards the island's peak again and again – moving right to left this time, left to right the next. As anyone who has climbed 'the Puffin' knows, the slope to the peak is steep enough and test enough for one climb. After three or four, it becomes a bit of a punishment. After six, I was feeling sorry for the pair.

Lunchbreak was the saviour. And a substantial sandwich lunch it was – for the film crew, for dad and son – and even for the boatman! But then came the *pièce de resistance* – filming dad and son tucking into their Weetabix.

'Cut! Cut! Cut!' Again and again, they munched great helpings of the cereal; again and again, the shot was not right. 'Cut! Cut! Cut!' This director seemed to be emulating David Lean – on a Weetabix budget! I do not know how many Weetabix the unfortunate pair consumed on the slopes of Puffin Island on that summer afternoon, but I am guessing that this particular cereal would be off their real-life breakfast menu for many a long day – perhaps forever! I never saw the finished advert; perhaps Puffin Island was as far as it went.

An Italian documentary crew, filming on Skellig, left strange impressions too. With much ado, this party wanted everything laid on – they even wanted this captain's company on the island to show them the best shots and angles. I led the director on a merry reconnaissance to all the favourite scenes that I had been photographing all my life – Small Oratory overhangs,

South Peak terraces, vertical cliffs, and precipitous falls ... until he took me aside and told me that these places were much too hazardous for the camera crew. I left them to their own devices at that stage, and returned to my sea-level colleagues, mouthing little surprise that Italy had not won a war since Caesar quit.

A French camera crew of May 1994 were quite the opposite. They wanted to do every crazy thing. But when I heard that their script included lowering an actor by rope from Skellig's South Peak to go swimming in the wild waters of Blue Cove some 217 metres below, I prevailed upon to them to take their ideas elsewhere.

A welcome contrast – and totally without fuss – was a visit by an American crew, shooting a Skellig component for a *Tommy Makem's Ireland* TV series. I landed them on Skellig pier in conditions so fine that I could spend all day tied up there, writing two long letters to my girls. The only disaster of the day was that my writing pad and its two splendid letters got 'lost overboard' on the way home!

Nobody visits the local Lemon Rock. Devoid of wildlife by the fact that Atlantic storm waves wash high over its 70-odd feet, this relatively tiny spike of old Devonian sandstone, dwarfed by its nearby Skellig sisters, also had a moment of movie fame when a scene from the BBC TV series, *The Ambassador*, was shot there on a fine autumn day in September 1998.

No: actor Pauline Collins was not appearing here in person in her screen role as the British Ambassador to Ireland. These were related scenes in an episode about the ongoing political détente between the Republic of Ireland and the UK over the ownership of the distant crag, Rockall. The Lemon Rock was Rockall's 'stand-in'. And the 'action' involved an activist painting an Irish tricolour on the rock – and subsequently baring his bum to a Royal Naval warship! And no, again: the Royal Navy was not present at the Lemon Rock either; that scene would be cut in later.

Nor was it my job to land the stuntman on 'The Lemon'; I had the camera crew and director on board the *Béal Bocht,* and a helicopter would carry out the landing operation. While I admired the courage and agility of the artiste who was prepared to grope his way around Lemon Rock, finding footholds on ledges where a petrel could not perch, the real star of the episode would never appear in the movie. This was the helicopter pilot who managed to achieve the landing on The Lemon's inhospitable peak, by holding the aircraft in place, with only one landing wheel touching the sheer crag, while the 'activist' scrambled out with a flag in his waistband, pots of paint in his hands – and his life on the line!

Retrieving the painter when the shot was done was a repeat of the pilot's artwork, and his aerial *pièce de resistance* back at the shore base in 'The Glen' was the successful round-up of a herd of cattle that had broken out of their farm as a result of all the noise and action.

For one day in late April 1996, I was back in the Special Effects Department of movie life again. Not quite *Ryan's Daughter* activity, this was a very mundane exercise, with two 'smoke machines' on board the *Béal Bocht* keeping a cloud of smoke wafting across Knightstown pier while some scene or other was shot in the murk. For every change of wind, my position changed accordingly, and even though I was never more than 200 yards from the pier, I could see nothing of the action that was going on in the smoke, and I have no idea of what the project was all about. But the celebratory 'crew dinner' in the Huntsman Restaurant in Waterville that evening – with sole-on-the-bone as big as a dustbin lid – was a good indicator of success.

The mobile phone rang.

'Mr Lavelle?'

'That's me.'

'Mr Des Lavelle?'

'Yes, indeed.'

'You're the man who does the Skellig trips?'

'Right.'

'I'm ringing you from Dublin.'

'I know.'

'How did you know that?'

'I see your number in the cell-phone display.'

'Oh … Can you tell me something about the trip? We may be coming to Kerry soon.'

'We do the trip daily – subject to the weather of the day – leaving Portmagee at 10.30am, spending about two-and-a-half hours on Skellig and getting back to Portmagee about 4.30pm.'

'Is there something to see on the island?'

'Well, there's the old monastic site from the sixth century, and of course the seabird colonies are quite world-famous.'

'You mean like seagulls and stuff?'

'Well, near enough.'

'Do all the boats go at the same time? I was speaking to Murphy and Casey…'

'If you were speaking with Murphy and Casey already, why are you talking to me now?'

'Oh, Mr Lavelle; I'm just looking for information…'

A 1990s poster advertising our boat-trips to the Skelligs.

'Well, after all that phone conversation, you must surely have enough information by now! Why don't you read my book? The current edition is called *The Skellig Story*. It's published by the O'Brien Press of Dublin and is available in any good bookshop – even in Dublin. Do give me a call when you've made up your mind. And now I wish you good day, sir!'

It was August and I had some real clients waiting...

Early TV – or even radio – shoots involved great cargoes of enormous equipment and great crews of helpers to cart the gear about, but one production on Skellig in May 1990 involved the most hardware and the most helpers I had ever seen on the island up to that date. This was a live BBC broadcast from Skellig – the first of its kind. Two boatloads of personnel and equipment were delivered to Skellig landing, and two helicopter-loads of equipment were delivered directly to the monastery area. Further personnel and signal-boosting equipment were stationed on Valentia's Bray Head. On a Sunday morning in May 1990, the sensitive presentation of modern monks chanting their psalms within the confines of the Skellig monastery readily conjured up visions of similar pious voices of a thousand years ago.

By any comparison, the crude, latter-day rape of Skellig's soul by *Star Wars* must stand indicted.

Pat and I took two days off in August 1999. One was to attend the birthday party of (Uncle) Jack Lavelle at the Royal Marine Hotel in Dún Laoghaire, and the second was to attend the birthday party of (Uncle) Jack Lavelle at the Royal Marine Hotel in Dún Laoghaire! Yes: with pressure of business, I had mistaken the date. The first trip yielded nothing more than some disappointing Dún Laoghaire sandwiches – and a quick trip home. The second trip then became an attendance at a fictional wedding of a fictional cousin that we had met at the birthday party. Otherwise, my colleagues would have scoffed for a week at the nonsense of taking two trips to Dún Laoghaire for the same session. Today, twenty-one years later, I can take the banter – if needs be.

Day-to-day boat work was interesting – if testing – in every decade. Salmon fishing in the 1970s/1980s was a frustrating exercise; the men of Donegal had been doing it for generations, and the men of Dingle and West Kerry had become rich on it years before the prospect of drift-netting for salmon at sea dawned on us in Valentia. There was no current tradition of salmon fishing in our area, largely because an ancient bye-law banned it in that area of the Kerry coast between Dunmore Head (near Slea Head) and Dursey Island – essentially all of Dingle Bay and Kenmare Bay.

On further inspection, the bye-law was faulty in itself as the areas it specified were too ill-defined, but while our new-found activity was thus legitimate, there was a catch: staying within the law meant using only a 'cloth' net of specified length, depth and material, which I did, and despite testing every spot in the ocean from south of Bolus Head to west of Inishtearaght, both by day and by night, I failed to accumulate such riches as those who had miles of illegitimate, sixty-mesh-deep, monofilament gear. I soon quit that pursuit.

But then I wrote a stage show about it all – *A Fishy Tale* – and a resurrected Valentia Dramatic Society produced it in St Derarca's Hall in Knightstown at some now-distant date that neither I – nor the few remaining performers – can recall. Perhaps it was 1980. The script was *of* the time and *for* the time, but as a coastal topic the theme may find echoes in any age. (Interested readers will find it reproduced in full in an appendix to this book.)

Mackerel fishing was an autumn activity through October and November – and it was a worthwhile exercise in the 1970s/1980s when fish were plentiful indeed, and a daily catch of forty or sixty boxes became the norm. Only short, economic journeys were involved – less than an hour from home to reach the fishing grounds – anywhere between Culloo Head, to the west and the Doulus Head 'Birds' to the east, where drift nets would be anchored on the surface at night or weighted with stones and anchored on the bottom by day.

Hauling them was the difficult part, particularly if the fishing was good. On one occasion, in 1979, on the north face of Doulus Head, my catch of mackerel was so great that it was quite beyond the capacity of the *Béal Bocht's* crew – Seán Murphy, Liam Musgrave and myself – to haul the fish-laden net, and we had to enlist the assistance of the passing trawler, *Spailpín Fánach,* and borrow her crewman, P.J. Sullivan, to help bring the catch on board.

But this was hardly a profit-making operation either. Though it totalled some 265 boxes of mackerel – a record catch for the local drift-netting operations of the era – the labour of removing 21,200 fish, one at a time, from each individual mesh, was a truly backbreaking torture that no money could relieve. My nets were also rendered to such unusable rags by the sheer overload that I had to scrap the lot and begin again.

Scallop fishing in the midwinter months was even nearer to home – within the confines of Valentia harbour. In earlier days, this work had been done in a two-man rowing boat, towing a steel scallop dredge along the bottom by means of an onboard, hand-operated winch, but by the time the *Béal Bocht* entered the Valentia fleet, onboard hydraulic machinery was doing most of the hard work, except for the final, laborious act of each tow – lifting the dredge and its load of fish, mud, stones and seaweed onto the gunwale of the boat. This was still being done by hand and by backbreaking exertion.

It was in these 1980s – on tourism promotional visits to the Netherlands and Belgium to advertise our newly developed diving-holiday services – that I noticed how the Dutch fishermen of Zierikzee had their mussel-dredging operations down to a much finer art. Their machinery did *all* the work and, using robust derricks, their winches could deliver the entire catch – and its associated rubbish – directly to an onboard table for sorting. I returned to Valentia, full of this new, labour-saving idea, only to be laughed to scorn. 'No need for such elaborate gear,' everyone said. 'It works fine the way things are.'

However, 'the way things were' did not suit my long back, and before long, with the aid of a few scaffolding poles as a derrick, I put the Dutchmen's ideas to work. Suffice to say that if you viewed the Valentia scalloping fleet in the following winter seasons, derricks or 'gallows' were in evidence on every vessel.

More sombre 'evidence' of those times was floating daily in Kerry's waters – the wreckage of the bombed Air India Flight 182, off Sheep's Head, County Cork, on 23 June 1985. In the following weeks, buoyant fragments of the aircraft had drifted as far as the Skelligs, and they were being picked up daily and brought ashore.

Among many other fragments, I recovered a toilet door. The most searing memory that has stayed with me to this day, and which somehow amplified and personalised the horror of the disaster, is the fact that the latch on that door was in the 'engaged' position.

Meanwhile, in those 1980s, there were opportunities to be pursued as a freelance harbour pilot. This was a service that had grown appreciably without any great promotion on my part since 1 August 1968, when the Kerry County Council appointed me to the 'temporary, non-pensionable' post of Knightstown's Harbour Constable. 'Harbour Master', I preferred to call it, since 'Master' was a more understandable title amongst the international seafarers who would be the target clients.

The wage for my 'Harbour Master' post was too derisory to mention. On the other hand, my duties – between my appointment in 1968 and my

The arrival of the Russian cruise ship, *Lyubov Orlova*, provided some activity for my well-soaked disinfectant mat during the foot-and-mouth outbreak of 2001.

resignation in 2005 – were equally so.

One session of Harbour Master activity came with the foot-and-mouth outbreak of 2001 and the need to maintain disinfectant mats on Knightstown pier to ensure decontamination of the shoes of any disembarking international visitors. As can be imagined, unannounced international, seaborne visitors were few and far between at Valentia in those days, but the arrival of the Russian cruise ship, *Lyubov Orlova*, and her eighty American passengers, on 30 May 2001, was one occasion to register some activity, as the visitors dutifully trod on my well-soaked disinfectant mat before setting out on a brief coach tour of Valentia's sights.

By evening, the *Lyubov Orlova* was gone to sea again. The next time we would hear her name was in 2013 when she was discovered drifting in mid Atlantic – unmanned, derelict and abandoned – having broken free under tow to a breaker's yard. Eventually, she was assumed to have sunk some

1,300 nautical miles from the Irish coast when signals from her EPIRB were picked up.

Strangely, that 2001 outbreak of foot-and-mouth disease increased my Skellig boat trip traffic. Numerous tourists who had signed up for Irish hill-walking visits now came to visit Skellig as it was the only 'hill' that was open. On the other hand, how many potential international visitors cancelled Ireland totally because of the disease, I will never know.

One Harbour Master duty that might be labelled 'activity' was the chore of supervising the installation of visitor moorings provided by the County Council in the harbours of Sneem, Caherdaniel, Portmagee, Valentia, Kells, Ventry and Ballydavid in 1998. This was not a *Béal Bocht* job; the great anchors and related chains weighed tons and called for the services of Mike Benison of Dingle and his substantial steel-built trawler. As a joint operation, it went well.

My subsequent job of collecting the £5 mooring fee from summer yachtsmen who availed of the Valentia buoys added only marginally to the Harbour Master's 'income', but it provided an insight into the financial psyche of a good cross-section of visiting sailors: their willingness to pay the fee was clearly in inverse proportion to the value of their vessels! Even though the scheme was well known and in use throughout the harbours of the south-west, from Sneem to Ballydavid, for several summers, few yachtsmen took the initiative or made the first approach to me regarding payment for the Valentia Visitor Mooring facility. All the others had to be accosted for fees – if they had not already succeeded in slipping quietly away in the dawn.

Eventually, the inevitable ageing of the Council's mooring buoy chains to a state of unreliability and the Council's tardiness in replacing them left me in the position of collecting fees for unsafe moorings. That was when I quit.

Effectively, pilot services were the only enduring benefit of the great 'Harbour Master' experience. In the 'old days' – and that was before my time

– there was considerable local competition for the provision of pilot services for the rare arrival of a visiting ship. There is even an old story of one boatman carrying a colleague in a sack on his back to a particular rendezvous in case 'the opposition' – on seeing the two together – might conclude that there was a pilotage job in the offing and steal the thunder.

In truth, pilotage was never a compulsory requirement in Valentia harbour, and all vessels had the option of doing their own inshore navigation, but even in the 1970s, some still came without the necessary local charts or nautical publications; they were happy to pay for local knowledge and assistance. An onward journey – by the Fertha river to Cahersiveen, for example – was a more complicated matter, and well beyond the capacity of first-time visitors, particularly since the channel was not buoyed, and most of the river's 'marks' were inconspicuous in the extreme. One had even been obscured for numerous years by a growth of trees.

A cruise ship in the harbour in 2019. Small cruise liners were regular pilotage clients throughout my time as Harbour Master.

All this boat-work was seldom a solo effort. Seán Murphy – himself a skipper of long experience in ferries and fishing – became a regular part of the *Béal Bocht*'s activity. Equally, in the early days, as a full generational circuit advanced, Jack Condon – son of Musketeer John and Marguerite Condon – joined the *Béal Bocht* as soon as school holidays came around each year. In latter days, 2007, when my wife, Pat, became ill, skipper John 'Kav' Sheehan joined the *Béal Bocht* and took many onerous duties off my shoulders. But throughout, skipper Mickey 'Dore' O'Connell was my inevitable pilotage hand, and he too could handle the *Béal Bocht* better than myself!

Small cruise liners such as the *Polaris, Clipper Adventurer* and *Caledonian Star*, landing up to 100 passengers to do a half-day's coach tour of a sector of the Ring of Kerry – from Renard Point to Sneem – as part of a round-Ireland cruise were much appreciated and enduring, regular, pilotage clients throughout that era.

Much goodwill ensued. On 22 July 1998, 'Mr Pilot' and his wife were invited to dine at the Captain's Table of the *Caledonian Star*, because the ship – which Mr Pilot brought in at noon – was not sailing until midnight. The best of food and the best of wines were on the menu at the Captain's Table, but Mr Pilot – with a midnight sailing looming – dined well but drank nil. A new wreck at the Perch Rock might make a great dive site, but better that somebody else would provide it!

Nevertheless, it was a splendid event, with much exchange of conversation with the passengers – many from US cities that we had visited on earlier 'Skellig' lecture tours. Later, when 'Mr and Mrs Pilot' had gone ashore in their dinner finery, Mr Pilot and Mr Pilot's assistant, Mr Mickey 'Dore', returned to the scene in their normal deep-sea garb and sent the *Caledonian Star* safely on her way.

On another occasion, as the *Caledonian Star* left Valentia en route to Sneem to collect her bus-tour clients, two new passengers were on board:

Pat Lavelle and John 'Musketeer' Condon were exclusive guests for a tour of the sights of Kenmare Bay.

Many of the pilotage clients were passing cargo ships of foreign denominations, needing only a temporary stopover during some inconvenient gale. Others might be foreign fishing vessels, forced to visit for some mechanical or diving service. Others were particularly regular visitors through the1980s. Small cargo ships – the *Richard C, Jessica B, Kay L, Marc L, Claudia L, Quo Vadis, Scott Trader* and the *Daunt Rock* – exported thousands of tons of forestry logs out of Cahersiveen until November 1990, when the Kerry County Council forced the enterprise to move elsewhere by declaring the weight and the height of stacked logs inappropriate for the Cahersiveen pier. I already had my own stack of 'exported' logs at home by this time.

On 14 August 1986, when the *Daunt Rock* ran into some unexpected swell just outside the harbour, a heavy list to starboard forced her back to reorganise her load.

On 14 August 1986, the *Daunt Rock* ran into some unexpected swell only a mile or two outside the harbour. Her deck-cargo shifted: tons of logs spilled overboard and a heavy list to starboard forced her back to the harbour to reorganise her load. Waste not, want not! As soon as she was safely berthed at Renard Point pier, I headed back to the accident area and loaded the *Béal Bocht* with enough of the flotsam to keep me supplied with firewood for several winters.

All these pilotage operations were in summer season only, and they were over-and-done with before the general public had even heard of the action. However, a planned new Cahersiveen Marina project had received considerable advance publicity in October 1999 when a tug delivering a barge for some preparatory work broke down at Church Island and had to be towed to its destination by Valentia lifeboat. In March 2002, news of the delivery by sea of a number of pontoons for the marina caused much publicity and excitement.

The scale of this operation and the size of the delivery ship had grown bigger day by day until the populace at large expected the *Queen Mary* – or, perhaps, the *Titanic*! People even believed a rumour that the ship was so big that she could not get into Valentia harbour and would have to be unloaded in Dingle Bay.

The truth, of course, was less strange than the fiction. The *Bavaria* was a standard cargo ship. I brought her into the normal anchorage north of the Valentia Lifeboat Station; the pontoons were offloaded into the water and were towed to Cahersiveen. But the crowds that turned up at Knightstown and at Renard pier to watch the event were reminiscent of a regatta-day assembly – or of the multitudes that had crammed the same vantage points some years previously when half of South Kerry fell for an April Fools' Day scam, perpetrated by newsman Pádraig Kennelly, that Fungi the Dolphin had quit Dingle and turned up in Valentia harbour.

On that occasion, Kennelly was aided and abetted by Radio Kerry, by a local Garda sergeant warning people 'on air' not to go to Renard pier because the 'Point Road' was choc-a-bloc with traffic, aided further by an accomplice boatman in Dingle, similarly 'on air', bemoaning the loss of Fungi, and by one Des Lavelle, 'on air' from the *Béal Bocht*, providing live commentary on Fungi's imaginary gymnastics near the Bar Buoy in Valentia harbour!

Distant influences were always at work in the shipping world. The fall of the Berlin Wall in 1989 eventually opened the Baltic Sea and Eastern European ports to visiting ships and won away many of the coastal cruises – from me, from the local vendors of fresh supplies, and from the coach-tour services and souvenir outlets of the Ring of Kerry.

However, even without the fine onboard breakfasts and good fees, it was a pleasure to be involved with passenger ships that were bringing people *into* Valentia harbour. Previous noteworthy vessels, the *Furnessia* and the *Belgravia,* had come to the harbour to *take away* almost a thousand emigrants in June 1883.

My pilotage experiences were not all 'coffee mornings and Danish pastries', though. The cargo ship, *Mull*, of some distant 'Georgetown', gave me some tough moments on the night of 28 March 1986. The *Mull* was a rust bucket; she was travelling light, her propeller and rudder half out of the water, and nothing on board working. But I did not know all this until later.

The story began when she was outside Valentia harbour in the dark of night, with an onshore wind, a weather forecast of worse to come, and an urgent need to get into the harbour for shelter. My colleague, Diarmy Walsh, with his boat, *Agnes Olibhéar*, put me on board the *Mull* – and my predicament slowly developed.

Only then did I notice that the *Mull* had no radar. Only then did I notice that she would not answer to the rudder except at full speed. Only then did

I notice that the Valentia leading lights – that should guide me safely past the hazard of the unlit Perch Rock – were extinguished. There was no room to turn the vessel out to sea; the wind was getting up; and I was on a roller-coaster ride to Valentia harbour, whether I liked it or not. I did *not* like it at all! And I liked it even less when the *Agnes Olibhéar* broke down and could not stand by the Perch Rock to show me an alternative guidance light.

Somehow, I got the *Mull* safely into the harbour and headed for the anchorage.

'Stop engines,' I ordered. But this did not change the pace; the *Mull* was now flying before the westerly wind like a great galleon.

'Slow astern!' Still, we lurched onwards.

'Full astern!' It made not a bit of difference; the propeller, only half submerged, was as useless as an eggbeater.

'Let go anchor!'

Nothing happened; the anchor winch was as rusted and as unworkable as everything else in the vessel.

The sandy beach of Beginish Island was coming to meet us. In truth, it was a welcome sight as it finally put a stop to the seemingly endless flight of the *Mull*. I was never so happy to be 'shipwrecked' in my life. And the *Mull's* Pakistani skipper was equally happy to be anywhere but outside on the open ocean with a westerly gale at his back and the hungry rocks of Basalt Point staring him in the face.

Eventually, the *Mull* was towed off the Beginish sands by Joe Shea in his Cahersiveen trawler, *Rónán Pádraig*, and when assorted sledgehammers and crowbars finally got the *Mull's* anchor winch to work, she rested safely in Valentia harbour for the duration of the gale. This was when I discovered that not only was she deficient in every item of equipment, but she was also deficient in funds. I never got paid for my exciting experience.

But Joe Shea did – in kind. Somehow, the coil of heavy, expensive cable that the *Mull* had provided for the tow off the beach remained on board the *Rónán Pádraig*.

Not all visiting vessels needed a pilot. Certainly, the fleet of the Commissioners of Irish Lights did not, and Musketeer Colin of yore came back into our Valentia lives by this route. Having qualified in his cadet school of the 1950s, and having done his sea-time in every capacity on every ocean and in every distant port of the world, he was back in Ireland, first in the role of Junior Second Officer on the lighthouse service vessel, *Isolda*, and later as Captain of the *Granuaile*. And every time Colin dropped anchor in Valentia harbour, he also dropped in on us for old-time chats. And what chats they were: Colin remembered every 'old days' pursuit we ever undertook, and he had a storytelling style that captivated even Céline and Linda for hours on end.

Indeed, it was his storytelling capacity that enabled him to draft his brilliant, three-volume work – *An Irish Periplus* – that would cover every mile and every service to every lighthouse and every navigation buoy on the coast of Ireland, almost to the detail of every related onboard conversation – warts and all, where relevant!

What might be called a few *Béal Bocht* 'warts' come to mind as well. On 14 July 1978, upon my return from Skellig, a garda appeared on the pier and 'busted' me for carrying more than twelve passengers. I have no argument with the facts; the garda's headcount was correct. But it might also be labelled a rather selective 'bust', as other boats of the Skellig fleet were landing at the same pier in the same hour in the same 'overloaded' state but they were not visited by any garda.

From memory, the event cost me £50 in the Cahersiveen court; but – also from memory – the day showed some profit nonetheless!

In truth, organising an exact, twelve-passenger complement was difficult – particularly when the frequent occurrence of 'no-shows' was a norm in the pre-internet, pre pre-pay arrangements of the times. In this context, I am reminded of a client whom I shall call Nanou.

Nanou came (on the phone) with recommendations from a moneyed house in Tralee. That, in itself, was not necessarily a bad thing. But Nanou herself was an overpowering, over-talking, French lady with a hint of aristocratic genes – real or imagined. She provisionally booked two seats for my Skellig trip a few days in advance and got my usual instructions – that she *must* phone a confirmation before 7pm on the previous evening.

Nanou did not confirm by the 7pm deadline, but ample bookings were coming through anyhow from the shoals of other fish that were in the sea. So far, so good! But Nanou was not gone yet; she finally phoned, at some late moment, and confirmed two places.

'Fine,' said I, in my most aristocratic English, for the aristocratic Nanou spoke the Queen's English better than any Kerry boatman. 'See me in Portmagee tomorrow morning.'

The phone rang again; it was Nanou, of course. 'I want to change the booking to three places,' she said.

'Fine,' said I again – not realising that I had already reached my complement of twelve passengers.

The phone rang yet again; Nanou had forgotten the time of the appointment.

'Eleven o'clock at Portmagee pier,' I told her, now beginning to worry about the concept of a passenger overload.

'Oh, but that is so late; I want to be the first on the island and to climb all those steps and feel the monks all around me in the morning...'

'Fine,' said I again, thinking now of Skipper Dan and his 10am departure and the fact that he had vacancies, and the serious fact that I had more than enough clients already. 'There is the possibility of a 10am boat, and I'll see what I can do about that.'

'*Formidable!*' In her excitement at having her way and winning a 10am departure, Nanou momentarily lapsed back to her mother tongue. But she promptly corrected herself: 'Wonderful … and I want to see your wonderful book and read all about the wonderful place, and all about the monks…'

'Fine,' said I. 'You'll be travelling in a bateau called the *Christmas Eve*, and I'll see you in time for your 10am sailing.'

The morning was pouring rain. At 9.45am, I found Nanou – resplendent in the most fashionable of rainwear – taking morning coffee in the Fisherman's Bar and regaling all and sundry with details of her wonderful life in Paris – at which all present were dutifully impressed and open-mouthed.

'Ah, Monsieur de Lavelle, I need to know so very, very much about the Skelligs and the islands and the monks, and I shall have so many, many questions to ask you as we sail along the way.'

'But you are not sailing along the way with me; you are sailing on the *Christmas Eve* with Skipper Dan. He sails at the 10am departure time that you requested; I sail at 11.'

'But I want *you*.'

'That's what all the girls say to me, but my wife doesn't like it a bit!' But my line was wasted on the crestfallen Nanou.

'I am so very, very unhappy that I cannot share the voyage with you, nor walk the steps of the Skellig with you as my guide…'

'But captains don't go on the island with guests anyway; there are guides on the island for that. And now your boat is waiting…'

'I shall have to come back … Oh, what a misunderstanding! I shall come back in the winter and I shall come and speak with you about all those Skellig questions.'

'But, Madame, I'll be in California in the winter.' This concept seemed to be quite beyond Nanou's grasp, and I did not pursue the point. 'And Monsieur Dan is now waiting for you.'

Collective mouths in the pub were fully agape by now, and perfectly good pints were gone flat and morning coffees gone cold as a consequence.

Nanou and her colleague stood up.

'Where's the third member of your party?' I asked, slightly taken aback.

'Oh, I forgot my phone and I could not inform you that we are now only two.'

Now it was my turn to be dumbfounded – not by Nanou's dismissive attitude, but by the looming vision of Captain Dan's sad face when I would deliver one client short of the quota.

But God intervened in the form of Captain Pat-Joe, whom I bumped into on the pier. 'Christ, Pat-Joe, have you one spare client anywhere?' I asked.

'One?'

'Yes, one.'

He disappeared behind a pile of lobster pots and pulled out a rain-soaked specimen whom he had quarantined there earlier for just such an occasion.

With much relief, I led my trio to the *Christmas Eve,* Nanou now with the demeanour of an 'aristo' being led to the guillotine in revolutionary France. I stood there happily in the downpour as they sailed off into the west, then, with a light step, I prepared my good ship, *Béal Bocht*, for her 11am departure and her precise complement of twelve clients.

Keeping within the law in various boating spheres was often difficult – especially if the particular law was ambiguous or the nature of the offence was vague. On such an occasion, upon returning from a long day at sea over a June bank holiday weekend in 1977 – including a Skellig visit, some diving and some angling with old friends Eamon, Jerry and Pierre – a garda appeared on the pier and boarded the *Béal Bocht*. He searched the boat and removed a bag of fish. Tight-lipped, we said nothing!

A full three months elapsed and the same garda visited me privately and gave me cash to the value of the confiscated goods. Again, I said nothing – except 'Thank you'. And that was the end of that.

With hindsight, I often wonder if the activities of the visiting cargo ships or passenger vessels of the 1980s and 1990s – particularly the regular callers – were confined solely to holds full of logs or cabins full of passengers. One day, when Mickey 'Dore' and I had just taken a laden cargo ship out of Cahersiveen and returned on the *Béal Bocht* to Knightstown, a gang of scruffy gentlemen suddenly materialised on the pier and jumped on board.

'Customs and Excise,' said one individual, with a scowl.

'Show me your Commission,' I said – because I was not going to welcome any visit by this grubby-looking rummage crew without identification. They dutifully produced their documents and proceeded to search the *Béal Bocht* from stem to stern. They found nothing. There was nothing to find. And I still don't know what they were looking for.

I trust they did not suspect this boatman of anything more sinister than a dabble in duty-free drink.

The Daffo-bills

I wondered should I scream aloud,
While wading through a bale of bills.
I thought of the Ansbacher crowd
With flowing-over money tills.
And here was I, upon my knees,
Asking which creditor to please.

The Cayman vaults are deep, for they
Hold loot that is taxation-free.
A working man could only pray

To join such jocund company!
Amazed and dazed, I sadly thought
What lack of cash my life had brought.

Contiguous with the stars that shine
In glossy magazines each day,
The players gild a monied line,
Kinsealy to the Kerry Way.
Ten thousand they would view askance.
A million gets a second glance.

But oft when in Returns I lie
To save a sou for fun or food,
It flashes on the inward eye,
The bliss of fiscal rectitude.
And then my heart with terror fills,
And trembles with Tribunal chills.

12

LIFEBOAT DAYS –
AND NIGHTS

Once upon a time, I thought that the Valentia lifeboat of the Royal National Lifeboat Institution could not get on without me. But time itself took care of that illusion, and the lifeboat service in Valentia is still very much alive and well, long after my departure from that young man's scene. Once upon an earlier time, though, in 1956, it seemed that the local lifeboat station might have to close for lack of crewmen, and in response to a general appeal, I became seriously involved for the first time, eventually progressing from the lowly status of seasick deckhand of the late 1950s to the more taxing duty of Second Cox'n from November 1969 – and onwards into the 1980s. Overall, it was a window into another aspect of island life; there were lessons to be learned, and the earliest were the hardest.

One of those early lessons came at 12.45am on 7 February 1959. The French trawler, *Marie Brigitte* of Concarneau, ran into the Foze Rock at the extremity of Kerry's Blasket Islands and sank within fifteen minutes. It is easy to know now that the position relayed to Valentia lifeboat – 'Three miles south of the Blaskets' – was misleading. In local parlance, that term could indicate anywhere south of the Great Blasket. Not until dawn of the following morning did we learn that the Mayday call referred to 'three miles south of the *Blasket lighthouse*' – Inishtearaght. The other French trawlers that hastened to assist read this location correctly from the outset, and only when they began reporting debris near the Foze Rock did the location of the disaster-site become clear to all searchers.

Eventually, we picked up two bodies – roped together with makeshift life-jackets of net floats. The memory of endeavouring to perform direct mouth-to-mouth resuscitation on two cold, lifeless, unknown, unshaven seamen, laid out on a rolling, heaving, windswept, spray-lashed deck in the darkness of a February dawn is not easily forgotten. All the textbooks we had read, all the lessons we had shared in water-safety classes conveyed nothing – absolutely nothing – of the real-life, nauseating horror of the situation.

On 6 July 2017, a French gentleman who had been only four years of age when his father died in that *Marie Brigitte* disaster, almost sixty years before, came with his family to pay a visit to the Valentia Lifeboat Station and to place a memorial wreath on the sea by the Foze Rock where we had picked

A water-safety class at Valentia in 1960. I'm kneeling at the front.

up his father's body in its makeshift life-jacket in February 1959.

The loss of the Irish trawler, the *Sea Flower* of Castletownbere, at the mouth of Ardgroom harbour in Kenmare Bay, at 1.21am on the morning of Sunday, 22 December 1968, was another failed lifeboat mission. We now know that the *Sea Flower* had gone down even while we in the lifeboat, *Rowland Watts*, were still some ten miles short of the disaster area; and I shudder just to wonder what we could possibly have achieved anyhow in the foaming cauldron that was Kenmare Bay on that occasion. The sea conditions on that night have gone down in my memory as totally dreadful. The 33-mile journey was bad enough, but the worst moment of the storm would hit Kenmare River, outside Ardgroom harbour, at dawn on the following morning. The lifeboat mounted a wall of water and literally *fell* into the next trough. It fell and fell, almost to the bed of Kenmare Bay some 20 metres below – there to be totally buried in water and green darkness as the following breaker crashed down.

Five good men were lost with the *Sea Flower,* but the sad event also offered a lesson. Long before the alarm was finally raised, there had been indications that something was amiss, and had the lifeboat, or the trawler *Árd Béara* that also came to assist, or other search-and-rescue services received timely notification, the outcome just might have been different. The clear lesson to be learned is this: when there is 'something wrong with the picture' in seafaring situations, it is better to alert the appropriate agencies in good time – better to risk the embarrassment and the nuisance of a false alarm rather than say nothing and allow a disaster to develop.

Good outcomes are always welcome. In a timely intervention by reserve lifeboat, *A.E.D.*, under Cox'n Jerh O'Connell, we evacuated an injured seaman safely from the Panamanian tanker, *Dona Myrto*, at midnight on 22 July 1956. Likewise, as a timely intervention, we put a doctor and nurse on board the British tanker, *Harvella* of London, at 4am on 28 May 1957, and eventually took the casualty safely on board the lifeboat, *A.E.D.*, about 15 miles west of Valentia.

On a similar service, on 16 October 1967, under Cox'n Jack Sugrue on the lifeboat, *Rowland Watts*, we put a doctor on board the 9,000-ton, German cargo vessel, *Ginnheim* of Bremen, to attend to a seaman's injury – and retrieved him later in the most foul conditions some four miles NW of Bray Head.

But there was never a guarantee of a happy ending. On 15 August 1974, in response to a request for urgent assistance for a badly injured seaman on a Spanish trawler – in position 52°12' North and 11°30' West – we set out in Reserve Valentia lifeboat, *City of Edinburgh*, in what the Returns-of-Service Book calls 'very rough seas'. With some eventual shelter from Inishtearaght, Cox'n Dermot Walsh put Nurse Mary Dromey and myself on board the trawler – Nurse Mary to attend medically, while my humble Spanish would assist with symptoms and medical history. Alas, there was nothing to inter-pret, nothing to administer; the casualty was already dead. Nurse Mary and I remained on board the trawler and headed to Valentia harbour – a dole-ful, two-hour trip in the company of fifteen very solemn, sombre, Spanish seamen.

Nor was it always medical passengers who accompanied us on the life-boat. We took a fire brigade to sea once – members of the Cahersiveen bri-gade, together with a portable pump – to assist the fishing trawler, *Spailpín Fánach*, which was making water rapidly near the Great Blasket island at 9pm on 7 February 1975. The trawler was already well down by the bows when we arrived on the scene, but the Cahersiveen firemen – now dressed in our life-jackets and forgetting their bouts of seasickness – pounced upon the *Spailpín Fánach* with their portable pump as readily as if she were a road-side casualty. Dingle firemen were also involved in the action, having arrived on the trawler, *Assumpta*. With pumps eventually keeping water-level under some control, the *Spailpín Fánach* was taken in tow by the Caheresiveen trawler, *Pato's Wish*, and the whole entourage headed for Dingle – which was reached safely at 2am.

Fortunately, not all the Dingle publicans were in their beds at that hour, and some considerable amount of hair was let down in James Flahive's quayside establishment – relieved fishermen in firemen's hats, sea-weary firemen in lifeboat life-jackets, and contented lifeboat men who were happy with another mission completed. What with songs, recitations and associated relaxation, it was 6am before our lifeboat, *John Galletly Hyndeman*, finally reached Valentia harbour – and home.

April 1972 saw another lifeboat mission with two additional, unconventional passengers. Press photographer John Cleary and journalist Tony Meade had joined us at 11pm on 5 April as the *Rowland Watts*, under Cox'n Dermot Walsh, headed to a remote rendezvous timed for 6am on the following morning, to evacuate a seaman who was seriously ill with peritonitis on the German factory ship, *Erich Weinert*. The rendezvous position was 51°30' North, 10°40' West – about 20 miles south-west of the Bull Rock – and the gentlemen of the press might have picked a better occasion than a night of 'gale and rain from the south-west'. In the event, it was an endurance test that would last for twelve hours and would see not only the journalists, but also most of the crew seasick and weary in the extreme. And all to little avail. By the time we had reached the original rendezvous, the *Erich Weinert* had amended the coordinates to a position some six miles south of Dursey Island, and by the time we got there, the helicopter, *Rescue 53*, guided by an RAF Shackleton aircraft, had already completed the evacuation. We never even saw the *Erich Weinert*; we did absolutely nothing for the sick casualty, Helmut Sranzen. And for his night's trouble, John Cleary got only a photograph of Valentia Bridge.

Nonetheless, Tony Meade managed to write a sensitive journalistic cameo of this great non-event – including his own reaction to Cox'n Walsh's offer of rum and dry biscuits as a pick-me-up in a cold, wet, hungry, seasick dawn. His account was published not only in *The Kerryman* but was even copied as far afield as New York.

It would be four years – 8 May 1976 – before we returned to the Bull Rock area, but this time with a little more success. Brendan Copeland, a member of the lighthouse staff, had become ill, and as no helicopter was available to do the evacuation, the *Rowland Watts,* again under Cox'n Dermot Walsh, stepped in. With our boarding boat in tow, we set out from Valentia at 16.05 GMT.

Bull Rock's two landing places offer poor comfort in any weather; and when a westerly swell charges through the island's great arch and is met at the East Landing by a similar swell breaking around the North-West Point, anyone of a superstitious disposition could well begin to believe the folklore that the Bull Rock – or Teach Duinn – is really 'The House of the Lord of the Dead'.

But the May daylight was in our favour. Even though the lifeboat could not approach the landing itself, five of us – with four oars – managed to keep the boarding boat in position beneath the 'man-derrick' as the lighthouse keepers lowered their ill comrade into hazardous space, and finally, albeit with a thump, into the heaving boat. Brendan was happy to be heading for medical attention, we were happy to put as much distance as possible between ourselves and 'The House of the Lord of the Dead' before night-fall, and Garnish Bay in Kenmare River beckoned as the nearest, convenient landfall. However, we oarsmen who then ferried the casualty ashore in our boarding boat to his waiting ambulance in Garnish spent rather too long searching for appropriate 'stores' for our long homeward journey.

Cox'n Walsh, who meanwhile had to contend with the hazard of a verita-ble lattice of anchored mackerel-nets all around the lifeboat, was not amused.

A sombre atmosphere, appropriate for Teach Duinn folklore, accompanied the *Rowland Watts* all the way home.

Some lifeboat trips, however, can be enjoyable outings – when neither life-saving nor storms are the order of the hour. Such are lifeboat deliveries – widely regarded as the pleasurable payback for real services in real emergencies. One such delivery – taking the *Rowland Watts* from Valentia in County Kerry to the Buckie Boatyard on the east coast of Scotland in 1977 – fell to me. It was the longest trip I ever had in charge of a lifeboat. *Rowland Watts* was nineteen years old then, and this was but another of the many boatyard appointments that kept her always in mint condition. She had, after all, covered many Atlantic miles since her ceremonial naming and launching at Knightstown, Valentia, by Mrs O'Kelly, wife of the President of Ireland, Seán T. O'Kelly, on 29 May 1958.

Now, on an equally fine day in June 1977, with John Curtin, Jimmy Murphy, Eoin Walsh and Noel Power, I set out from Valentia, with scheduled fuelling and rest stops planned along the way. Kilronan in the Aran Islands was our first port of call. After a ten-hour trip, this was a welcome layover. It was also an opportunity to exchange notes with old lifeboat colleagues of the Kilronan station and to appreciate again the classic cliff scenery of Dún Aengus – and the islanders' equally classic chiselled faces that made *Man of Aran* and its characters so powerful and so unforgettable.

Mayo hospitality awaited us in Achill, where helpful friends guided us through the Sound and through the island's swing bridge, and even treated us to a conducted tour of the local beauty spots – from sea level at Keem Bay to the island's highest point of Slievemore.

However, that was all we saw of Mayo, for a thick fog shrouded our morning departure, and even when we encountered a disabled salmon drifter off Annagh head and made a detour to tow the vessel into Frenchport – a creek that seemed scarcely wider than the *Rowland Watts* – we saw nothing of that haven except the radar image. A fine salmon from the generous Mayomen was a more than adequate recompense for our fog-bound visit, and the thought of large, fresh salmon cutlets helped us on our way, promising a welcome alternative to the standard emergency fare of lifeboats in those days – self-heating cans of tomato soup, tins of corned beef, tins of dry cracker-biscuits, tins of cigarettes and bottles of rum.

In her day, the *Rowland Watts* sported a motley array of culinary machinery: a Primus stove of another century, a frying pan, a whistling kettle and a 12-volt electric kettle that might boil water in a week – if at all. But what she lacked on this particular cruise was a chef. And much of the splendid salmon – half-boiled, half-fried, half-raw and totally ruined – was promptly re-consigned to the Mayo waters from which it came.

The thick fog on this calm June day in 1977 also denied us a view of nearby Eagle Island. This was a disappointment to me, and a planned visit there is still unfulfilled – to see a lighthouse station that, more than any other on the coast, has borne the brunt of every westerly gale and suffered the ferocity of every storm-wave that stems from the island's proximity to the 100-fathom line and the format of its western cliffs.

It is also a lighthouse station full of Lavelle history. This is where my paternal grandmother, Elizabeth Healy, daughter of lighthouse keeper Matthew Healy, was born in 1882; this is where my Lavelle great grandfather, John, served as Principal Keeper during the worst storm of several centuries which hit the island on Friday, 29 December 1894. The events of that storm are best captured in excerpts from an article, 'Green Seas at Eagle, 1894', which appeared in the lighthouse magazine, *Beam*, volume 7, no. 2, and drew heavily on a letter from Polly Ryan who – in an era when entire families lived in the lighthouses – was staying with her brother, Tom Ryan, in the East Station:

Eagle Island East, Belmullet.
January 1st 1895

My Dear [Sister] Kate,

... I told you of the gale...But Friday the 29th beats all. What would you think at half past two to jump out of bed and into water? ... Green seas were going over our houses ... when we got up to see the door broken down and the rooms all filled with the sea ... the Lantern was out ... window frames, roofs and all the house was going to pieces ... The slates were being lifted off like flies. The youngsters were all brought downstairs as the sea was coming down on their beds ... the windows all broken in, the staircase carried away ... the paint and oil stores were levelled to the ground ... The men from the Upper (West) Station came down between the sprays ... and took us one by one to their station to Mrs. Callaghan and Lavelles ... and we were thankful to God to reach them....

Your loving sister, Polly

And it was at this hard station too that the next generation of Lavelle lighthouse keepers – my grandfather, Peter Lavelle, born in 1873 – also joined the lighthouse service. Indeed, if I examine the generations of Lavelles that served in lighthouses on the coast of Ireland and the generations of Healys and Lavelles that served as seamen and sea-captains on two oceans – and even on the Great Lakes of America – I may finally find the source of my permanent addiction to boats.

Today, Eagle Island is uninhabited, and its one remaining lighthouse has, since 1988, been unmanned, automated and powered by solar panels – a far cry from 1841 when the island's census noted two lighthouses and seven dwellings.

In any case, we cruised onwards through the calm June seas of 1977. Aran Island in Donegal was another overnight, with spare time for an evening walk over familiar countryside where, on an earlier visit to Aranmore lighthouse, I had coursed the same fields in pursuit of wintering geese, and had learned the solid logic of the expression 'a wild goose chase'!

This was our jumping-off point for the Western Loughs of Scotland and the Sound of Islay – a ravine where even a lifeboat needs a favourable tide to master the fierce streams en route to Islay's Port Askaig, itself a place where a visiting boatman needs an abstemious disposition to master a tour of some seven distilleries. Suffice to say that the next time I spied the full range of Islay's products and their evocative labels, rooted in the island's Gaelic placenames – *Lagavulin, Ardbeg, Laphroaig, Bunnahabhain, Bowmore, Caol Ila, Bruichladdich* – it triggered good memories. That experience was thirty years later, though, and six thousand miles away, in the Chieftain Bar at the corner of Howard and 5th in San Francisco.

That would be in a different life, in January 2008. In June 1977, we still had a lifeboat delivery to complete, and steaming onward from Islay, another day's trip brought us into Fort William at the foot of Ben Nevis and to the entrance to the Caledonian Canal. Sixty miles of waterway, including three loughs, twenty-nine locks, and twenty-two miles of canal proper, took us through the Great Glen of Scotland to Inverness on the Moray Firth, and a further short day saw us at our destination in the Buckie Shipyard on the Banffshire coast of the North Sea. Beautiful indeed – every inch and every hour of a week-long trip – but the most remarkable oddity of the entire journey was at Inverness rail station; nowhere else in the world have I ever seen an assembly of so many totally drunken men in one place at four o'clock on a Friday afternoon! Clearly, Scotland's ancient strong drink was flowing as freely as Scotland's newfound North Sea oil. Indeed, these gents' happy state of anaesthesia was greatly envied by one of our crew. On the deck of a boat, he would face the Atlantic in winter gales, storms, or worse, but now, the mere thought of our imminent plane ride homewards across the Irish Sea on a fine June day could reduce him to rubble.

There were no flights involved in another lifeboat delivery trip, but we did take a rather interesting – if circuitous – route home. This was the delivery of the reserve lifeboat, St Andrew, from her station of Portrush, County Antrim, to a maintenance boatyard in Crosshaven, County Cork. It was 1977. The political situation in the North of Ireland was an unhappy one, and a previous lifeboat stop in Portavogie in County Down, en route to Portstewart, County Derry, had been stressful for us Southerners. The answer this time was to take to the high seas, make no further overnights in the North, and head southwards via Scotland and the Isle of Man.

But there had to be one final Antrim diversion. Islanders all, we simply had to pay a courtesy call to Rathlin Island, which lay right in our route. And we did. We tied up alongside a small pier in Church Bay for a brief visit – so brief that none of the island's main attractions were on the agenda, not even that peculiar Rathlin-West lighthouse with its lantern sitting at the foot of an 18-metre tower rather than on top. Not even McCouig's nearby pub was on the agenda. Instead, we stretched our legs for half an hour and chatted with a sociable quayside gent who may well have been 'the King' of this legendary place – legendary, in the sense that Rathlin had an export industry in stone axe-heads more than 5,000 years ago; legendary, in the tale that 'Bruce's Castle', near the present Rathlin-East lighthouse, was the hideout where Robert Bruce, through watching a spider's repeated toils, regained sufficient self-confidence to return to Scotland and to his historic victory at Bannockburn AD 314.

There were other legendary, non-contentious Rathlin seafarers to be discussed on that fine summer's morning at Church Bay – namely the Viking visitors of AD 795, Sir Francis Drake of AD 1575, and even the Marconi team that made its first wireless broadcast here in 1891. But in marine terms, the most legendary aspects of Rathlin – of which shipping is still well aware today – are the savage tidal currents, rips, and over-falls that plague Rathlin Sound. Veteran sailor, Saint Columba, learned this almost at the cost of his life in the virtual whirlpool of Slough-na-More off Rathlin's Rue Point as he journeyed to Iona in the sixth century. Earlier still, Brecain, son of Niall of the Nine Hostages, lost a fleet of fifty boats in the same maelstrom AD 440. Indeed, it is worth noting that even in March 1986, the Irish Lights tender, *Granuaile* – no stranger to these waters – was swept 90° off course by the same tidal phenomenon.

But we had a journey to make. The tide was in our favour; a gentle breeze did not even ripple the notorious Rathlin Sound, and we left this island 'kingdom' of one hundred souls and headed for Scotland.

Portpatrick on the Mull of Galloway was a placename that had long been imprinted in my head during many previous long hours at sea in Valentia lifeboat on Atlantic waters: Portpatrick Radio, that powerful Scottish marine communications station, would come blasting in over the airwaves on 2182 kHz – even in 'blind spots' like Kenmare Bay where Valentia Radio, scarcely thirty miles distant, could hardly be heard. However, as to Portpatrick itself, I was a novice. Pilot books and charts notwithstanding, the entry to this tiny harbour – a virtual cleft in surrounding high cliffs – was daunting in dark of night when harbour lights, domestic lights and vehicle lights combine to confuse the weary seafarer. But the welcome was worth the worry. In this outpost, which is variously described as 'the farthest west you can go in southern Scotland' and 'the farthest south you can go in western Scotland', local hospitality – be it western or southern – made us feel at home. And for a typical lifeboat-men's gathering in this region, the inevitable night-long topic had to be the disastrous North Channel storm of 31 January 1953 and the consequent loss of 132 lives in the sinking of the car-ferry, *Princess Victoria*.

However, the morning's light and the promise of an interesting day's journey to destinations south soon dispelled such sombre considerations. The scenery, likewise, as we headed seawards again, was a joy to any islander's eye. The surrounding hills could well be the gorse-covered coastal ranges of Kerry, and the great aerial masts of Portpatrick Radio towering above the sea-cliffs of the Mull of Galloway could well be the masts of Valentia Radio towering above the sea-cliffs of Dohilla, on Valentia Island.

Port Erin on the west coast of the Isle of Man was our next planned destination, but the weather took a hand in the proceedings. As the cruise wore on, a westerly wind soon became a north-westerly gale that followed us down through the North Channel, and reached its height in just the wrong place – west of the Isle of Man. A lee shore in those conditions was not an option; Port Erin was out. We continued our southward run, past the Calf of Man, and it was here that the combinations of wind and tide were at their worst – mountainous following seas that seemed determined to swallow us or break into our exposed aft cockpit at every swell.

It was a great test of the lifeboat – a small, underpowered vessel, already almost at the end of her days. But with a drogue trailed astern for stability, and her twin 35-horse-power Weyburn engines throttled back, *St Andrew* – already credited with saving twenty-one lives in her career – brought us five safely through also, albeit with some anxious moments. We rounded the Chicken Rock lighthouse, edged eastwards into the shelter of the Calf of Man, and set a course for Port St Mary on the south coast of the Isle of Man.

I had a cultural mini-mission in the back of my head – to find someone who could speak the Manx language so that we might compare a few notes with its Irish counterpart. But I was already some years too late. I was told that the last real 'native' speaker, Edward Maddrell of Glenchass, had passed away in 1974. Not entirely content with this information, and accompanied by my staunch crewmen, I continued a tour of several of the Isle of Man's pubs in pursuit of the ancient tongue, and even if a late-night bar with much music and dancing may not have been the optimum place for language studies, we did learn that '*Slaynt vie*' in Manx is the equivalent of '*Sláinte mhaith*' in Irish – and we seized every opportunity to repeat the phrase many times thereafter into the late hours before we finally said, '*Slane lhiat*' or '*Slán leat*' or simply goodbye.

Indeed, it is worth noting that for anyone visiting the Isle of Man today, the language quest should be easier; in the census of 2011, some 1,823 people claimed to be able to speak, read or write the Manx language – '*Y Ghailck*'.

Ten hours steaming from Port St Mary saw us in Dún Laoghaire and ensconced in the luxury of its Royal Marine hotel, where the splendid quality of the Steak Diane promptly entered the annals of lifeboat fare – and the substantial cost of the dish promptly exceeded the lifeboat delivery crew's meagre travel budgets.

Another day's sailing saw us in Rosslare harbour, a place better remembered for the hardship of an earlier lifeboat-delivery visit in a northwest gale so foul that we were unable go to the pier to refuel. Luckily, on that occasion, the Irish navy minesweeper, *Fola*, was equally stormbound at anchor in the bay, and we were glad to impose upon her generosity for enough diesel fuel to see us as far as Arklow.

Rosslare waters invariably evoke tales of local, high-profile marine incidents, foremost amongst them the loss of the cargo ship, *Flying Enterprise,* in January 1952, when – following a week of heroic salvage efforts in dreadful conditions by the deep-sea tug, *Turmoil* – Captain Kurt Carlsen, Master of the *Flying Enterprise,* made world headlines daily as he refused to leave his disabled and listing ship. Equally in the limelight was Kenneth Dancy, First Mate of the *Turmoil,* who joined Carlsen on board the sinking freighter until the bitter end, when both of them had to jump from the horizontal funnel of the stricken vessel – to be picked out of the water by the *Turmoil* four-and-a-half minutes later as the *Flying Enterprise* went down.

It's not that I was part of this event in any way. I was not even in the lifeboat service then. But I had heard the story a dozen times, for my father had been stationed on the Tuskar lighthouse in 1951 and had been in the thick of all the related radio communications of the *Flying Enterprise* saga, from start to finish.

Many disasters from other ages linger in Rosslare waters – and anyone with lighthouse-service connections may dwell on the dreadful storm of 1821 that cost ten lives when the temporary wooden cabins of the Tuskar lighthouse-builders were washed into the sea. But even if a passing seaman's concern on a fine day on this coast is the simple matter of getting the timing right to gain a few extra knots from those testing tides of Tuskar and Carn-sore, a passing lifeboat man may do well to dwell also on the wild waters that can well up here. The 1914 wreck of the cargo ship, *Mexico,* on the Keeragh rocks – and the loss of nine Fethard-on-Sea lifeboat men in a rescue attempt – is an adequately sobering thought.

The approaches to Dunmore East – from any direction – are dominated by Hook Head lighthouse, and I set a course that would take us within a stone's throw of this landmark. This was not just for curiosity; it was not just to view this most ancient lighthouse that dates from the early thirteenth century – and traditionally relates back to St Dubhán of some six hundred years earlier.

For me, sailing close inshore past the Hook was a trip down memory lane that I was not prepared to announce or share with my crew. It was here on St

Hook Head lighthouse dates from the early thirteenth century.

Dubhán's ancient signal post that Pat and I had become engaged on a summer's evening some twenty years previously.

That was too private a memory. And my colleagues' very predictable retorts would have broken a special spell, would have crushed memories of Hook's mediaeval tower, of its dimly lit, vaulted internal chambers, of the 155 spiral steps to the lighthouse balcony, of the burnished brass of the light's winding mechanism, of the blinding incandescence of the light's glowing mantles…

Instead, the conversation drifted to a safer topic – the nearby wreck-site of the British trawler, *Merchant Vanguard,* also of 1956 – and to the fact that the current onboard inventory of my own *Béal Bocht* included a dividers and compass that my father, when he was Principal Keeper at Hook Head, had snatched from the same *Merchant Vanguard* shortly before she finally succumbed to the hungry rocks of 'The Hook'.

The day's trip down, Dunmore East – haven of many lifeboat journeys – was a welcoming destination. But my enduring memory of Dunmore East has been neither food nor accommodation-related – but rather the splendid state of cleanliness of the harbour's public toilets! This discovery was a rare experience anywhere in 1977.

The trip's final leg, into Crosshaven in Cork harbour, completed quite a luxury tour, and also completed my circumnavigation of the island of Ireland. The remaining south-coast section, from Valentia to Cork, had already been traversed several times in uneventful trips, with little of note other than experiencing an occasional, welcome upgrade in coastal accommodation options – quite a far cry from some earlier lifeboat deliveries when the travelling crewmen from Valentia Island were obliged to sleep three-in-a-bed in some questionable hostelry on the coast of County Cork.

A State Reception in Dublin Castle, on 4 March 1974, to celebrate the 150th anniversary of the founding of the Royal National Lifeboat Institution was a splendid opportunity to meet and exchange notes and experiences with many colleagues from the marine rescue services. But I met one particular colleague who was reluctant indeed to share any thoughts or reviews of a rescue mission in which we had both participated some months previously, on 24 August 1973. I was the lifeboat Cox'n on the *Rowland Watts* on that occasion, and he was the pilot of an army air corps rescue helicopter.

Some of the story of that August mission can be gleaned from the Returns-of-Service-Book of the Valentia Lifeboat Station:

At 0900 GMT, Marcue [Marine Rescue Coordination Centre, Shannon] reported by telephone to the Hon. Sec. that a Greek cargo ship required assistance – seriously injured crewman on board – position approx. five and a half miles Northwest of Skelligs Rock. [Lifeboat] 938 [*Rowland Watts*] slipped her moorings at 0930 GMT. Coxswain Walsh was away for the day, and 2nd Cox'n D. Lavelle was in charge. 938 reached the casualty at 1300GMT and the sick man was taken off the cargo ship. Air Corps helicopter transferred the injured man from 938 off Bray Head to hospital in Tralee…

That is the official part of the story. Those of us on the *Rowland Watts* saw more detail. We met the cargo ship in very calm conditions at the appointed position; the injured seaman was lowered over the side of the ship in a stretcher; he was received securely onto the deck of the *Rowland Watts* with no difficulty, and we were already halfway home when the helicopter arrived to rendezvous with us at sea for the speedy onward transport of the casualty – an operation that had been well practised for smoothness and efficiency by both participants.

It should go like this: the lifeboat steams into the wind at about 6 knots; the helicopter keeps pace, hovering overhead. A 'winchman', carrying an appropriate stretcher, is lowered from the helicopter by cable to the boat's deck. The casualty is strapped – bound hand and foot, almost – into the stretcher. The winchman straddles the casualty, hooks the stretcher to the lifting cable and gives a thumb signal to the helicopter to 'lift'. And that should be the end of the story. But in this case, it was not!

The winchman gave his 'lift' signal, and he and the stretcher were lifted about three feet off the deck – and thumped back again. Another 'lift' signal from the winchman – another jerk, and another thump. A third 'lift' signal

An injured seaman being lowered to Valentia lifeboat.

– this time, the dangling couple soared into the air and away from the lifeboat. And then came the moment that my airman colleague did not want to discuss. The helicopter, complete with its human load still dangling at the full extent of the cable, began to lose height, and slowly the bound casualty was dipped into the sea – ankles, knees, waist. Not alone that, but the winchman could be seen scrambling up on top of the casualty's chest to ensure that he at least was clear of the ocean. For terrible minutes – or seconds, perhaps, that felt like hours – we thought we had a catastrophic helicopter ditching on our hands. But the moment passed, the helicopter struggled into the air, and operations returned to normal. To this day, I wonder if the unfortunate casualty needed much therapy – additional to his original requirements – for the shock of being nearly drowned in a straitjacket off Bray Head in full view of his would-be rescuers. I don't wonder at all that the helicopter pilot did not particularly want to re-live the event in the middle of a gala social function.

In distant days, before we had dedicated helicopters for rescue missions, the Valentia lifeboat worked closely with Britain's RAF Nimrod surveillance planes – modified versions of the Comet airliner – which were frequently called in for the typically large search areas of the south-west coast of Ireland. Eventually, I flew with those RAF men out of their base in St Mawgan in Cornwall. It was a familiarisation and liaison exercise, and it was quite an education for me in days when lifeboats – for want of funds, or reluctance to spend them – were lagging behind even the Irish fishing fleet of the day, particularly in matters of electronics and communications. It was the early 1970s, and there had to be security considerations in welcoming an Irishman into a British RAF base, but I received courteous services throughout – and experienced everything that this planeload of electronics had to offer as we took off to rendezvous on autopilot with a target buoy about 50 miles west of Land's End. 'What magic equipment,' I thought; 'Just punch in the co-ordinates, and it'll take you there.' We had nothing like that on the Valentia lifeboat of those times.

'Rocks! Rocks on the starboard bow!' This cry must be the most terrifying call that any captain, skipper or lifeboat cox'n ever heard since the day when men first went down to the sea. And that's exactly what my bowman lookout, Pat Curtin, was shouting to me in the thick of fog and the dark of night on 28 August 1970: 'There are rocks! There are rocks!'

'Stop engines! Full astern!' We came to a standstill. But there *couldn't* be rocks here; we should be in deep water, a mile west of Bray Head. It was one of my earliest services in command of the Valentia lifeboat, as I had been appointed 2nd Cox'n only a year previously. I was shivering; we *couldn't* be a mile off course? We just *couldn't*...

The service call had arisen in response to a report of a boat overdue in Ballinskelligs, and that's where we were headed. The lifeboat, *Peter & Sarah Blake*, had no radar then. In fact, apart from diesel engines and some radio equipment, she had the basic navigational aids that had changed little since Lieutenant Bligh left the *Bounty* in 1789 – a chart, a compass, a timepiece. Thick fog was everywhere on that night of August 1970, and the sea was as calm as glass. Already – in the same thick fog – we had left the Lifeboat Station and had nursed our way along the harbour shore to 'the Beacons', and then followed a compass course out of the harbour without ever seeing Cromwell Point lighthouse at the harbour mouth. Once in the open sea, we plotted a series of courses that would take us north of Valentia's 'Wireless Point', west of Bray Head, east of the Lemon Rock, west of Bolus Head, south of Horse Island and into Ballinskelligs Bay.

'Rocks! Rocks on the port bow now!' came another lookout's call. Even though we were on the same boat, I could hardly see him in the fog. And then, in some long, long seconds it dawned on us all that the 'rocks' in

Landing an injured lightkeeper from Inishtearaght.

question were a school of dolphins, not the least bit discommoded by the fog, and having much acrobatic fun at our expense.

We never did complete that mission; the overdue 'casualty' had already arrived safely back at his home. And I was more than happy to head for mine – only to have to turn the *Peter & Sarah Blake* about and head for the Inishtearaght to evacuate an injured lighthouse keeper. My fog-induced grumble that a basic navigational accessory such as a Walker Excelsior Mk.4 Log (for distance measurement) should be included in the vessel's inventory eventually had to make its way to the UK headquarters of the Royal National Lifeboat Institution before such a commonplace item was finally supplied.

A mission on 11 December 1976, which provided help in one situation and saw a loss of life in another, also initiated a certain benefit. We were already at sea in the *Rowland Watts* with Nurse Daly of Valentia on board to attend to a fisherman who had sustained crushed fingers on board the *Spailpín Fánach* near Inishtearaght. But then we heard a report that the *Saint*

Collette had lost a man overboard in the nearby Blackhead Sound. As soon as Nurse Daly was safely on board the *Spailpín Fánach*, and heading for home with her patient, we joined the nearby search effort – which included eight fishing boats and an Air Corps helicopter.

The young victim, John T. O'Shea, was never found. However, the small benefit that ensued was that the shockwaves of this local loss spurred South Kerry fishermen – particularly those who had never been able to swim – to undergo a series of basic swimming lessons weekly in the Tralee Sports Centre pool, under the auspices of the Irish Water Safety Association, with instructors David Slattery, Michael O'Regan and Noel Power.

Quite apart from the pool curriculum, time was usefully spent in the water, experimenting with the fact that a fisherman's wellington boot, rather than being something to be kicked off and discarded in a 'man-overboard' accident, can be used as a valuable item of buoyancy if it can be emptied and upended with air trapped inside.

Some lifeboat missions go down in memory as historic non-events, like the service of 12 June 1957, when, with great fanfare, the Commissioners of Irish Lights were initiating the concept of using helicopters for lighthouse relief. All was in readiness. Valentia lifeboat was standing-by at Skellig as security. But at 10.30am, a thick fog came in and grounded the aerial component of the big event. We grinned wryly on the lifeboat and headed home, content in our watery, foggy element, and expressing the common opinion of those 1970s that the boats and ships of the lighthouse service would never be replaced by these new-fangled helicopters.

But it was a theory too far, and the helicopter service would soon earn the respect and gratitude of even this initial sceptic. On 7 February 1974, I had volunteered to become a temporary assistant lighthouse keeper on Skellig, in place of keeper, Brian Regan, who had to be evacuated in urgent family circumstances. An easy trip to Skellig on Valentia lifeboat *Rowland Watts* and an easy landing by 'man-derrick' performed the changeover.

A week's work at Skellig lighthouse, spent cleaning things that were already clean and polishing things that were already shining, could hardly be described as 'following in the footsteps of my father, grandfather and great grandfather', who spent their lives in the lighthouse service and served in almost every station from Tearaght to Tuskar to Tory. Nor could the duration of my Skellig tour of duty match up. And nor could my eventual departure. When relief-day came – together with some considerably bad weather – and forecasts of further gales suggested an even longer Skellig stay, this 'temporary assistant keeper' was happy to forget about boats or lifeboats or lighthouse vessels, to pocket his scepticism and get a ride home by helicopter.

Lifeboat services – successful, sorrowful or inconsequential – are always rewarding. The trawler, *River Spey* of Milfordhaven, Wales, sprang a leak off Valentia's Bray Head on 28 February 1954, and we went to her assistance in Valentia lifeboat *A.E.D.* Not that the trawler really needed assistance as such; the after-cabin was flooded but so long as the bulkhead could hold, she was still able to continue steaming at full speed towards the safety of Valentia harbour – which she eventually reached with some time to spare. The lifeboat did nothing more than accompany the *River Spey* on her Valentia-bound dash, but in sharing a large mug of tea later with the trawler's cook, I was struck by just how much our company had meant to them.

'Do you know something, Paddy?' he said to me, as I studied him across the steaming brew. 'We're all bloody 'eathens, Paddy, but at times like this morning out there in the bay, even *we* start looking up pretty 'ard. I ain't got no God or Church, but when I saw your little lifeboat 'longside this morning, I looked up to the sky and said "Thanks" to Someone up there too.'

I too said 'Thanks' once when I was at the receiving end of a Valentia lifeboat service. It was 28 April 1993, and failure of a minor engine component left me and my *Béal Bocht* drifting with four passengers on board near the Small Skellig. No storm, no gale, no life-or-death situation; just a modicum of embarrassment in being towed home by the lifeboat – even if only once in forty years. There was also a modicum of consolation in the fact that the Cox'n and 2nd Cox'n of the lifeboat, *Margaret Frances Love*, on that day were Seánie Murphy and Richard Connolly who, respectively in 1972 and 1968, had begun their seafaring careers as my deckhands on the same *Béal Bocht*!

In the end, the most enduring memory of my lifeboat years is the memento that I wear on the ring finger of my left hand. It is not a band of gold or silver, but a weird, misshapen fingernail. The original went overboard with a lifeboat anchor chain in 1960. I could have gone with it. But I was agile in those days.

13

AMERICA – AND BACK!

I was on the *Béal Bocht*, about a mile south-west of Valentia's Bray Head, heading homewards from Skellig on a tranquil September afternoon in 2001, when my colleague, Eoin Walsh, called me on the VHF: 'Switch on the News,' he said. 'There's a plane after flying into a tower in New York!'

I immediately thought of Linda, Céline and Steve and family; even if they were 2,000 miles west of New York, they were still too close to such an event as this. Likewise, my passengers, shocked and shivering, feared the worst for friends and relatives near the disaster area.

Valentia

23rd September 2001

Dear Céline, Dear Linda, Dear Steve, Dear Sam and Dear Jackson,

I haven't attempted to write a letter for a while because I haven't yet recovered from the terrible world disaster of Tuesday 11th September 2001. I probably never shall. Nor shall anyone else in the world, for Tuesday was the day when horror fiction became real.

We need no longer look to outer space for enemy aliens; they are already here amongst us, and indistinguishable from ordinary humans.

They may look like us, and live and act like us in many ways, but alien indeed are the perpetrators of Tuesday's acts – alien in their warped minds and alien in their unfathomable hatred that has taken lives by the thousands, destroyed the lives by the tens of thousands and ensured that life will never be the same again for the tens of millions.

And the fact that it all happened an ocean away from me and that it was not visited on those I love is no relief. The prospect with which we must now live to the end of our days helps me to say things that are often left unsaid and share thoughts that are often left unshared:

I have had a long life – double and treble the time-span allotted to many of those victims of Tuesday 11th September. I have had a great life – uninfluenced by the fanatical causes and fanatical hatred that created Tuesday's terror. I have had much joy from my dear family; I am proud to be whoever I am, and proud and honoured to be loved by those who love me.

If it should happen that I meet an untimely end like so many innocent souls of recent days, or, indeed, if I should pass away sooner or later through less spectacular events, simple accidents or even natural causes, I ask that you should not be sad for my going, but that you should remember the lines and the sentiments of this paragraph. I shall say it again: I have had a great life; I am proud to be whoever I am, and I am proud and honoured to be loved by those who love me.

I was up this morning in the inky darkness of pre-dawn. I could see my way around the house and out on to the patio by the brilliance of a million stars in a clear sky. The sea below the house was silent, still and peaceful. Later in the day, I was at Skellig beneath a blue, blue sky and a calm, calm sea with some sweet, sweet people who loved and appreciated every minute.

As I wandered home in the evening's September sunshine, the fuchsia in full bloom was bursting from the roadsides in a great rush of scarlet and mauve enthusiasm. One might think that all was well with the world.

But it isn't. And we can't fix it. Yet this doesn't mean that we should begin living our lives in bubble-wrap or cotton wool. We must just carry on doing the little things that we do. We shall sail, we shall fly, we shall visit, we shall respect, and we shall love.

And we shall pray that those who do bigger deeds and think bigger thoughts may have guidance from a good God.

Much love, D.

From that 911 moment and from its consequences, a paranoid and security-ridden America would never again be the same for me. Fortunately, however, old impressions of the more mellow country that I experienced in the America of the 1980s and 1990s – now truly a lifetime ago and surely a galaxy away – still temper the harsh realities of today's international politics.

Pat and I were not just occasional visitors to the United States; since our girls emigrated there in the 1980s, we were partial residents, living there during autumn, winter or spring – sometimes for three months or more. For us, it was easy: as soon as Valentia boating matters were completed at the end of summer, we pulled the *Béal Bocht* up into dry dock, locked our doors and headed west – San Francisco initially, where Céline and Linda were based, and later including Butte, Montana, where Céline provided a home from home.

A Poem for Linda

Hey, Child! 'Tis surely time that you were born.
We've counted days and weeks and months till nine.
But you took no example from the norm,
And dared to do your own review of time.

Hey, Girl! Awaiting bus-time by the gate,
Self-breakfasted and scrubbed and set to go,
What inborn tempo keeps you up-to-date
And staunch to study all there is to know?

Hey! Teen-age kid! Why not some disarray,
Some wasted time, some idleness, some slack?
No! Year by year and month and week and day
You followed far a single-minded track.

Hey! Lady with a city at your feet,
Achiever, walking tall amidst the crowd,
As San Francisco marches to your beat,
We tap our toes to time and we are proud.

A chance meeting with the American novelist, Leon Uris, during a Skellig trip on the *Béal Bocht* in 1972, and several subsequent boating encounters in the 1980s, expanded our Valentia horizons and introduced us to the Irish American Cultural Institute's then programme of bringing Irish experiences – art, dance, music and history – to diverse audiences at diverse venues throughout the United States. This, in turn, launched me – an innocent in that country – on a series of slide-illustrated *Skellig Story* lecture tours through some twenty US cities in the period 1986–90.

Part of my innocence was in my movie-generated and fictional perceptions of America: I was naive enough to fear that everyone from New York to the Pacific coast was an Al Capone, a Badlands bandit or a hostile Indian. How wrong was that! I found no gangsters on my trail – no more, at least, than might readily be found in Ireland – and I was easily converted to acknowledging a very acceptable United States of America, full of good experiences and good people.

There was much innocence too in the Americans' history-and-folklore-generated perception of Ireland. To some, we still lived in thatched cabins, were still suffering from famine, and were all 'Freedom Fighters' who would shoot an Englishman on sight. It was an interesting – if politically charged – circuit, with opportunities to amend these ingrown misconceptions

San Francisco's famous Golden Gate Bridge. At every stop on our slide-illustrated *Skellig Story* lecture tours, there was a story to tell and a story to learn.

on both sides, and where I encountered an occasional 'Brits Out' or 'Up the IRA' comment, my frosty reaction surely sowed some seed of enlightenment on any ground that was at all receptive.

Much air travel was involved, and very promptly Pat and I began to understand the immensity of the American continent. One day, we could be in the frozen wastes of Duluth, Minnesota, looking out over a frozen Lake Superior towards an invisible but equally frozen Canada; next day, we could be viewing the Mexican border from the barren, blistered landscape of El Paso, Texas. One day, we could be gazing over the Atlantic Ocean from the cliffs of Newport, Rhode Island; a day later, we could be admiring the Pacific Ocean from the Golden Gate of San Francisco. At every extreme, and at many places in between, there was a story to tell and a story to learn – and much to be observed.

In Newport, Rhode Island, we – of humble homes – could admire at close quarters the magnificent summer 'cottages' that lined the three-mile Cliff Walk and its environs, virtual palaces that the rich and famous of New York's Golden Era of the 1800s had built for their leisure days. We gazed in wonder at such 'cottages' as *Belcourt Castle*, built in 1894 in the Louis XIII style; *Chepstow*, an Italianate-style villa of 1860; *Beechwood*, former home of Lady Astor, mother of John Jacob Astor IV who died onboard *Titanic*; *The Breakers*, a grand, 70-room, Italian Renaissance-style villa, built in 1895 by Cornelius Vanderbilt II, President and Chairman of the New York Central Railroad; *The Elms*, summer home of coal magnate Edward Berwind of Philadelphia and New York, modelled on the mid-eighteenth-century Château d'Asnières outside Paris; and *Château-Sur-Mer*, a mansion in High Victorian architecture, famous as the setting for an elaborate country picnic for over two thousand guests in 1857.

Contemplating the labour involved in such magnificent structures, we could also note – as did Bishop Fenwick of Boston during the construction of the Fort Adams harbour defences in 1827 – that some 150 Irish men were involved. In a more nautical vein, a Newport joy for this Kerry boatman was to put a finger in the dockside waters that had been home to that battle of sailing giants, The America's Cup, from 1930 until 1983, when the *Australia II* took the trophy and the venue Down Under.

An appropriate follow-up to Newport was a visit to the San Francisco boat show of 1990, and, suitably speechless, to admire the America's Cup itself – even if its spirit had been considerably tarnished by New Zealand's court challenge to the legitimacy of the USA's 1988 boat design. This 1990 boat show was also an opportunity to view Dennis Connors' *Stars and Stripes '88,* the catamaran marvel of space-age alloys, fabrics and fibres that had won that 1988 event – on the water and later in the courts – and had retained the trophy and the venue for the USA by easily outsailing New Zealand in San Diego on 7 and 8 September of that year.

The Golden Gate Bridge, Fisherman's Wharf, the Embarcadero… The

The Californian island of Alcatraz was a magnetic icon for this islander.

'must-see' sights of San Francisco are legion, but for this islander, the Cal-ifornian island of Alcatraz – scarcely a mile from the San Francisco water-front – was a magnetic icon from the outset. Tales of Al Capone, George 'Machine-gun' Kelly, James 'Whitey' Bulger, Robert Stroud (the Birdman of Alcatraz) and other notorious inmates who, in their time, were incar-cerated here had whetted my imagination even in childhood. Likewise the enigmatic 1962 disappearance from Alcatraz of convicts Frank Morris and the brothers John and Clarence Anglin who braved the cold waters and fast tidal currents of San Francisco Bay in a homemade vessel fashioned from raincoats, was – whether they 'made it' or not – a compelling interest.

Some sentiment for the Indian Nations' occupation of the island, 1969–71, was a further factor in my thoughts, as was the option of experiencing the inside of a federal penitentiary as a voluntary day-visitor, and 'escaping' from the island at my leisure on the afternoon ferry.

The visit did not quite live up to the mystique. Built as a defensive fort of the 1850s, Alcatraz served as a federal penitentiary from 1934 to 1963, and in 1990 many of its structures were still awaiting planned refurbishment as a visitor centre. But I came away better informed – particularly in the fact that the Birdman of Alcatraz was really the Birdman of Leavenworth, Kansas, as it was there, during his earlier incarceration, that Stroud's ornithological activities took place.

I also brought away an enduring impression of prison life: Robert Stroud's cell in Alcatraz did not have space for many canaries anyhow.

Our travels soon dispelled my common misconception that all Irish emigrants of the nineteenth century were famine-era émigrés. Many had American roots long before the famine, and in Glen Allen, near Richmond, Virginia, our hosts were happy – and proud – to display splendid, Irish-made furniture that had accompanied ancestors on pre-famine voyages from 'the old country'. This personal exhibit seemed to us a far more rewarding memento than the standard, decades-old, Richmond attraction – the period architecture of the old hotel where the 'stairway scene' of the classic 1942 movie, *Gone with the Wind,* was filmed. Indeed, an updated 'Deep South' experience was available on an Amtrak train journey southwards from Washington DC to Richmond, when overheard conversations and remarks – however jocose – told us that the American Civil War of the 1860s had never really gone away. We maintained a very civil *béal dúnta* on that topic.

The strains of 'The Boys of Barr na Sráide', played by three all-American violinists on an upstairs balcony greeted us in Pittsburgh, PA. We had not expected to hear so sensitive a rendition of Cahersiveen's signature tune some three thousand miles from home.

Pittsburgh University's 'Irish' Classroom is another memory landmark of that visit. Its architecture, structure, stained glass and carved-oak furniture are visible links to Killeshin Chapel, to the Book of Kells, and to such ancient centres of learning as St Finian's in Clonard, St Columcille's in Derry and St Carthage's in Lismore. The discerning visitor may also learn that the cornerstone – from the Abbey of Clonmacnoise – conceals a container of earth from both extremities of Ireland.

Phoenix, Arizona, was aptly named, I thought. As we flew in, the city seemed to rise up – not from its ashes, perhaps, but from a yellow inversion layer of smog, dust and smoke. Equally, the whole surrounding countryside, the largest irrigated area in Arizona, seemed to rise up in green from the all-encompassing desert. That was 1987. Phoenix is still green, still compulsively attractive for the thousands of northern visitors who winter there for its sunshine and warmth – a climate that offers only ten inches of rainfall a year, a climate where giant saguaro cacti, monuments to my boyhood Wild West fantasies, stand tall, from roadside to parking lot to surrounding arid hillsides.

But the Phoenix we saw in 1987 was a far cry from the original settlement that was won from the desert by the waters of the three rivers – the Gila, Salt and Verde. One thousand years ago, the Hohokam Indians had a perfect balance of hand-built irrigation canals and ditches for their agricultural cultivation here; nowadays, modern man's expansion into the desert, and drilling ever-deeper wells to reach the over-used and limited groundwater source, is described as a 'geographic hazard', leading to the collapse of the valley's natural infrastructure, subsidence in the landscape, rockslides, and the proliferation of dust storms on the winds that sweep in from Mexico.

In Phoenix in 1987, an attendance of 110 at my Skellig programme was a good indication of the Phoenix-like status that the city's Irish community enjoyed at that time – an ethos that continues today with their forefront position in Irish-language studies and the busy social usage of their splendid Irish Cultural Centre.

In nearby Scottsdale, a local Indian Fair, celebrating the culture of the Zuni and Navajo Nations, provided an added amazing sensation. Apart from their specialities of sand-painting, turquoise jewellery-making and tribal dances, the themes, characters and cultural messages of the Indian folktales could readily have come from our own Irish sagas.

We were again reminded of our Irish folktales in Cincinnati, Ohio. A fascinating family heirloom was an old manuscript, the saga of Fionn and the Fianna, handwritten in Irish, with many corrections and marginal notes. When I later brought home photographs of some pages of the manuscript, Dr Pádraig de Brún of the Institute for Advanced Studies identified it not only as a 'textbook' from Ireland's hedge-school period, but as the property of a particular schoolmaster, Willie Hayes, of Barracks Cross, Milford, Charleville, County Cork, who died in 1836.

In Duluth, in the winter of 1987, our fascination at encountering the novelty of a lakeshore piled high with ice was equalled by the unlikely mathematical odds of a chance meeting. This was with Sister Noreen, who had shared a desk with Pat's mother, Josie O'Shea, at the Cahersivane National School near Waterville, County Kerry, in 1916.

A further surprise awaited us in Los Altos, California. At the end of my lecture, 'Any questions?' brought a tall, white-haired man to his feet. 'In your book, *Skellig – Island Outpost of Europe*, you were wrong about my grand-mother's maiden name,' he said. 'She was Cahill, not O'Sullivan!' This was Walter Harrington, long-time resident of California, and the grandmother in question was a lady who in her youth in Portmagee, County Kerry, had worked on Skellig Michael as a teacher to lighthouse children. What could I say? Walter knew his granny better than I did. And when I assured him that the next edition of the book would do justice to Joanie Cahill – who later became Mrs O'Sullivan – he even supplied an appropriate photograph of her for inclusion in the reprint, and we wound up as permanent friends. Later, we would make many visits to Walter in San Francisco, and he would likewise visit us on Valentia – his most notable trip being when he and sev-eral colleagues arrived on our Valentia Island tennis court via helicopter as a break from an Irish golfing tour; our most notable visit to his world had to be the exclusive use of his Hawaiian condo at Kaanapali beach on Maui's La Hina shore during January 1998.

This Maui visit was the source of a strange flashback to absolute child-hood for me. Viewing the neighbouring Hawaiian island of Molokai some nine miles away across the wild Pailolo channel, I suddenly found myself back at a distant, childhood date when a speaker, lecturer, priest, proselytiser or fundraiser of some genre brought a show/lecture to Knightstown's St Derarca's Hall, and told – in harrowing terms – the tale of the missionary priest, Fr Damien, who, having gone to Molokai in 1864 to help the leper colony inhabitants, finally caught the disease himself. I must have been seriously under-age for exposure to that horrifying tale that lived some-where beyond memory for so long.

We did not venture to Molokai; the warm waters and gentle swells of La Haina beach entertained us well for mornings and afternoons, and the television coverage of the investigation into the affairs of one Bill Clinton entertained us indoors while we hid from the midday sun. Indeed, the much-used term 'inappropriate behaviour' sent me to the dictionary – to find that 'inappropriate' meant 'unsuited'. Eureka! Bill and a certain lady had not been just groping in each other's pockets; they were 'un-suited', or in nautical parlance, 'stripped down to the gun'ls' for their carry-on! The lawyers never pursued this line.

Nor did we pursue the TV too long; the midday view from our Kaanapali condo offered non-stop humpback whale watching, as the great beasts were in the peak of their migrations – Alaska to Hawaii, and back.

Throughout all our winter tours on the US mainland, the common denominator everywhere for my Skellig slide presentation was an auditorium of Irish Americans of the first, second, third or fourth generation, and, if attendance was a measure, Chicago's Irish-American Heritage Centre at 4626 N. Knox Avenue was an Irish beacon of note. Formerly Mayfair College, the Centre had been acquired only a year previously, and had yet to boast of today's fine library and museum. Nor was its 'Fifth Province' bar yet in evidence, this later catchphrase name arising from President Robinson's 1991 visit and her reference to Irish emigrants as being Ireland's 'Fifth Province'.

But with some 212 people from Ireland's four provinces crammed into the auditorium on that winter's evening in February 1988, Chicago's new Irish-American Heritage Centre was already a place to remember. And there were people to remember there too: Mary Murphy, for example. My age to within two days, she had shared classes with me as we tripped our way through the halcyon days of Knightstown National School on Valentia Island. Being kindred spirits in the 1940s, we had many common topics to review in 1988. I had seen her as the little girl whose mother had returned from America because of frequent and continued ill-health; Mary had seen me as the little boy from the Cable Station who had no real dad at home. We were waifs-in-common in a way.

And Mary finally answered a lifelong question of mine. How had she kept her school pencils manicured to the meticulous standard that we all envied in the distant era of Johnny Mawe's classes? It was simple: she had been the proud owner of an American pencil-topper; the rest of us had only razor blades – and rusty ones at that!

The waterfront of Lake Michigan in Chicago in the month of February 1988 was an impressive place to re-learn my neglected 'Temperate Climate and Continental Climate' geography lessons of Knightstown National

School and of the Sem. On a sunny February afternoon, Pat and I set out for a walk on the lakeside, and – Kerry sheepskin coats notwithstanding – the Windy City and its winds of minus 20° would soon have claimed our innocent lives were it not for the wisdom of our host-for-the-day, the then Consul General of Ireland, who came and rescued us.

Pat admires an ice sculpture in St Paul, Minnesota.

We might have suffered a similar fate in St Paul, Minnesota, where I had given a Skellig presentation at the College of St Thomas. The city's Ice Sculpture Festival was in full swing and was so exciting for us of temperate climes that we just stayed outdoors in our Kerry finery. Luckily, there was hot cider on hand to revive the innocent visitors.

Our hosts' hospitable home was also memorable for being the place where, for the first time in our lives, we learned to say 'Grace Before Meals' in Irish:

Beannacht ó Dhia mar a suímíd le céile.
Beannacht ó Dhia ar an bia atá rómhainn.
Beannacht ó Dhia ar na lámha a d'ullmhaigh dúinn é.
Beannacht orainn féin. Amen.

In San Antonio, Texas, the ubiquitous Durty Nelly's pub on the city's newly gentrified River Walk did not quite equate to rural County Clare. For me, with my childhood Wild West fantasies still to the fore, the Alamo, with its visions of Davy Crockett, Jim Bowie and Santa Ana, was the region's highlight. There was another 'old times' connection in San Antonio then, too, that I did not know about until a few years later. The Auxiliary Bishop of San Antonio – later, Bishop of the Diocese of Tyler, Texas – was none other than Edmond Carmody of Moyvane, County Kerry, who had joined the Sem with me as a lonesome pleb in the dim and distant days of September 1947.

Philadelphia, with its significant historical buildings of modern America's Founding Fathers, was not to be glanced at in one visit. Equally impressive was Chestnut Hill College, venue for our Skellig lecture. Nor could our local hosts, Bernard and Grace Croke, be categorised as brief acquaintances. The twin flags over their door – the Stars and Stripes and the Irish Tricolour – were much more than a political gesture to Bernard's Irish roots. This was a house that, in quiet, unpublicised connections with senior politicians, diplomats and ambassadors, did endless work for the Irish immigrant community – particularly the newly arrived, the fearful, and the lonely.

Our first visit was only the beginning of a long friendship. Bernie and Grace visited us in Ireland in 1988 and sailed to Skelligs with me on 16 September of that year. Later, in 1989, on what seemed to be the finest February day in New York's history, we visited the Statue of Liberty together – where I was happy to abandon the party and *climb* to the top, since, at 93 metres, it is only half the height of Skellig Michael! Another 'highlight' of those East Coast visits of the 1980s saw me leaving Atlantic City casinos with a *win* of TWELVE dollars! It was an enduring boast that would not be silenced until I lost it all – and a bit more – in Las Vegas in 2004.

The city of Rochester, in upstate New York, could be called Kodak City. For me, an interesting Rochester connection was its proximity to the fabled Niagara Falls.

Everything there seemed to lead to Kodak. Everyone there, it seemed, worked for Kodak. I was even careful to announce that most of my slides were Kodak – lest I be run out of town.

For me, an interesting Rochester connection was its proximity to the fabled Niagara Falls, but we spent only half a day on the Canadian side of the river; there, the priceless beauty of the winter-frozen falls is diminished by the area's dreadful architecture.

The other Rochester – in the State of Minnesota – saw the social side of our Skellig meeting almost turn into a medical conference. This is the home of the Mayo Clinic, and the Mayo Clinic is home to many young Irish doctors and related specialists. Architecturally too, the Mayo Clinic is something special to visit. Its various centres are linked by a warren of underground tunnels – a worthwhile consideration in a city where winter blizzards are the order of the day and where the outdoor temperature is in the minus range for much of the year.

In Springfield, Massachusetts – home of so many of the Blasket Island and Corca Dhuibhne emigrants of earlier years – the first real blizzard of our lives grounded our short air connection, but another Lavelle came to our rescue there. John Lavelle – no relation, even though my granduncle of the same name lived out his life as a seaman on America's Great Lakes – undertook to drive us to our next appointment. And he did – through snow and ice, past trucks and cars that were stuck in the roadside margins, he delivered us safely to our next appointment in Lowell, Massachusetts.

Lowell is a city that should be on anybody's educational tour of the industrial revolution period of the United States. Situated at the confluence of the Merrimac and Concord rivers, the original Lowell thrived on the water and the energy of the Pawtucket and Wamesit Falls that powered its cotton mills of the mid-1800s. Likewise, the water fed various canals – the Merrimac, the Cut River, the Jeremiah's Gutter and the South Hadley – linking various industrial sites with the sea at Boston from 1792 onwards. An interesting economic factor of that time was the high employment of young, unmarried, female mill-workers – the 'Mills Girls', as they were known – and the provision of convent-like accommodation for them. All are immortalised today in the Boott Mills building, which now enjoys a new life as a visitor centre and museum that re-tells Lowell's nineteenth-century industrial history in fine detail.

The area's beautiful Crane Beach is also taking its place in history, not just for its splendid sands but also for its importance as a wildlife refuge and a breeding ground for the piping plover – a species endangered to the point that now only some 1,300 pairs exist on the US Atlantic coast. Alas, the domestic pets of an ever-advancing human population pose a new and serious threat to this refuge. But if the visitor to Crane Beach thinks that its unusual access footbridge is somehow for the plovers' benefit, this is not necessarily so; it is to elevate the beachgoer safely above the surrounding grasslands and the hazardous, disease-inducing Lyme ticks that can be encountered there.

The brain-bank of Harvard and MIT notwithstanding, Boston, in the run-up to St Patrick's Day 1988, was rather predictable: tacky leprechauns grimaced in every window amidst an overabundance of 'Begob' and 'Begorra' and 'Erin Go Braugh'. But the ultimate Boston experience for me was to stand before the cathedral-like, 115ft-high gable of glass in the pavilion of the John F. Kennedy Presidential Library, and watch the endless caravan of shining aircraft – like some flickering perpetual flame to Kennedy's memory – following each other into Logan's runways, minute after minute and hour after hour.

Further views of America would follow when Steve Maloney of Butte, Montana, introduced Céline to his hometown. In a total contrast to the warmth, busy city streets and crowded highways of California, Montana

Céline and Steve Maloney on their wedding day in 1994 – an Irish/American wedding in the middle of the Rocky Mountains.

offered snow and mountains and empty highways for as far as the eye could see.

Soon, it also offered an Irish/American wedding in the middle of the Rocky Mountains on 7 January 1994.

I had a stereotypical picture in my mind of the standard wedding procedures, standard celebrations. I thought I had everything covered. But I did not know that this Butte wedding called for a peculiar Good Luck bridal accessory – an Irish horseshoe, an old one!

This left me searching a Cahersiveen stable yard at about 5pm in the dark of a winter's evening – the evening prior to our departure to join Céline and Steve, his siblings and extended family for the big event. All credit to the Cahersiveen stable-owner who found me on the premises, believed my story and donated the required item rather than calling the gardaí.

New York City's attendance at my Skellig programme in the Geological Society on E 58th Street in 1988 was a disappointment. Surprisingly, the local Irish organisation there was not on par with other centres. Nor did the city itself impress; my most interesting New York tour was a night drive with a retired policeman through the hinterland of Central Park and Harlem. The most memorable daytime event of that New York visit was spying, for the first time in my life, a notice that said, 'Pick Up After Your Dog!' In my Kerry of the 1980s, such an exhortation might be beneficial, I thought.

New York, in fact, had disappointed from my first US entry in 1986.

The immigration officer at JFK Airport had not impressed me with his people-skills. He was inclined to label me 'La Velle', instead of 'Lavelle' – and he did not like to be contradicted. It made me think of the many immigrants of old who had met a similar, gruff greeting a hundred years previously at Ellis Island or Castle Garden or, indeed, at any US immigration port from Boston to Philadelphia to Galveston, Texas. Fresh from the bowels of some coffin ship, the weary, timorous souls were probably happy even to be alive, and glad to tip their caps and agree with whatever name or corrupted surname anyone in authority might give them.

For us, US immigration desks – be they on the US mainland or later at Shannon or Dublin – were never happy occasions. Suspicion seemed to abound, leaving us with the impression – real or imagined – that access to the United States was some sort of privilege beyond our qualifications and that, as 'tourists', we were spending too much time in the country.

As a way around this limitation, Pat and I finally achieved 'Green Card' status on 11 June 1997 by presenting ourselves at the US Embassy in Dublin with our financial statements, birth certificates, marriage certificate, Garda references, health certificates from a designated doctor, and professional mugshots from a designated Dublin studio. I even had to produce my discharge papers from my FCA involvement of the 1950s to prove that I was not going AWOL from the Irish Defence Forces!

We believed that this new status would see us free to stay in the United States for as long as we wanted – largely to become wintertime babysitters for young Sam Maloney while his parents, Céline and Steve, completed their studies at the University of Montana, Missoula. But our Green Card idyll did not last for many visits. Soon we ran into further immigration-desk hassle because, as Green Card holders, we were spending too much time – (all summer long) – *OUT of the USA!*

As a consequence of such ongoing nuisance, we eventually voluntarily

Pat with Céline, Steve, Sam and Jackson in Butte, Montana, where we spent several winters on babysitting duties.

surrendered our precious Green Cards, resorted again to tourist status, and thereafter tailored our visitations to 'The Land of the Free' accordingly.

The Irish community in the city of Syracuse in upstate New York did not so readily 'tip their caps' to officialdom. This is the only city in the USA with a traffic signal where the green light is on top. The story tells that a long time ago, when traffic lights were a novelty, the Irish population of the Tipperary Hill district of Syracuse took exception to the fact that their new (1925) traffic light at the junction of Tompkins Street and Milton Avenue had the red and orange above the green. They stoned it, wrecked it, and amended the signal by hanging it upside down. The City promptly put it back. It was attacked again – and restored again. The battle raged until the City fathers eventually capitulated, and Tipperary Hill, in a great victory for Irish people-power, got to retain its unique traffic light with the green light uppermost. Not alone that; today there is a classic sculpture in place at that junction to immortalise the original protesters who threw the first stones at the offending installation.

It is only a stone's throw across the Rio Grande, from El Paso, Texas, to the Mexican town of Juarez, and our lecture visit in the Texan city in 1987 was not complete without a brief incursion into its Mexican counterpart. But half a day was enough to note at a glance the extremes of living standards on either side of the border. The shanty-town suburbs of Juarez boasted none of the comforts of the United States, and the mêlée of roadside vendors south of the border selling flowers and souvenirs to departing visitors was a measure of the attraction of a US dollar among people who had nothing.

Little wonder in 1987, and little wonder today, that the border, some 1,900 miles in length – and with or without a wall – has witnessed an endless stream of illegal immigrants from south to north. It is a matter that occupies much discussion in Congress and in the White House, with much reference to 'security'. Meanwhile, the great, obvious, and acknowledged truth is that the US economy – particularly its huge agricultural and food-processing components – would disintegrate overnight without the poorly paid labour of the Latino 'Braceros' from 'The South'.

The airport of Omaha, Nebraska, about as far from American borders north and south or oceans east and west as any place could be, was rather unique in 1988 – being awash with military personnel. This had nothing to do with Mexican immigrants, and nothing to do with land-border defences, but all to do with the fact that the Offutt Air Force base, some ten miles south of Omaha, housed the US Strategic Air Command's headquarters – charged with keeping America's then bogeyman, the Soviet Union, under watch. With a mobile workforce of 10,000 and some 24,000 family members and retirees, the military – and military-related – personnel of Offutt's B52 bombers, strategic nuclear weapons and intercontinental ballistic missile command made Omaha's civilian airport look as if a *real* war was in progress rather than a *cold* one!

Apple Valley in California never saw an apple – at least not in the area that we visited in February of 1987. Little wonder this: situated some 100 miles east of Los Angeles, Apple Valley, on the fringes of the Mojave Desert, boasted sand, Joshua trees aplenty, and tumbleweed, perhaps, but no apples. Indeed, not even houses were in evidence at that time. We stayed at No. 21345, Klamath Road, but numbers 1 to 21344 were nowhere to be seen. I have not returned to Apple Valley since then, but I'm guessing that an ever-widening Los Angeles commuter belt has seen fertile gardens extend eastwards amongst the Joshua trees and into the desert-that-was. I am also guessing that the 21,344 missing houses may now be in situ – and selling well at last, as I note online that no fewer than fifteen real estate offices are listed in Apple Valley now.

A 'Skellig Evening' in Los Angeles was the purpose of this 1987 visit to Southern California, and my being led into the LA venue by a kilted piper was the local organisers' way of ensuring a good evening's entertainment for the audience. But my own entertainment was to come a few days later in Anaheim's Disneyland – a place where, even amidst the unsophisticated illusionary tricks of 1987, any adult should be a child for a day, and not even try to figure out the magic behind all the shows and activities.

But Disney's 'Pirate Ship' perplexed me. As I watched it cruise around Treasure Island again and again, I could not understand or explain how the skipper could manoeuvre this ungainly galleon through its narrow canal and then dock it so perfectly each time without even a scratch. I would have had trouble trying to achieve this in my agile *Béal Bocht*. But the eventual answer was simple: the Pirate Ship was not floating at all; she was rolling through the water on underwater tracks. Disney's magic had blinded this child!

In 1988, however, I had good eyesight. Or so I thought, until I began photographing orchids in the home of Lynn and Bill Davis during our Skellig presentation in Tulsa, Oklahoma. These were not just 'snaps'; they were detailed macro-shots – almost inside the flower itself. 'Not much scent,' I thought, as my nose was about four inches from the bloom.

'Lovely orchids,' I commented to our hostess.

'Yes,' she said. 'They're silk; I made them myself.' My jaw hung open for a while; then I slunk off outdoors where I might make less of a fool of myself.

The Oral Roberts University of Tulsa was a striking reminder of the considerable riches that TV and radio preachers have won from their congregations here in the heart of the 'Bible Belt'. Likewise, the Council Oak Tree, sacred site of the Creek Indian Nation when they were driven west from Alabama in 1836 on the Trail of Tears, is a poignant reminder of the continent-wide saga of treaties made and treaties broken. But, if it's any consolation, Tulsa's Gilcrease Museum is a fine memorial to the culture, dress, art, ceremonies and lifestyles of the Kiowa, Comanche, Lakota Sioux, Osage, Arapaho and Cheyenne Nations.

Las Vegas! Anyone should visit Las Vegas – and for no more than a weekend! I had to wait until January 2005 for my first opportunity, and until 2011 for my second, and – even if I came home with a few dollars less – I came home with enough impressions to constitute a veritable 'Litany of Las Vegas':

Litany of Las Vegas

Las Vegas is a veritable desert of red rocks and sand somehow made habitable by the engineering genius of the Hoover Dam.

Las Vegas is a place where any tourist with any inclination towards sanity should be locked up on arrival for their own safety while the other 35 million annual visitors engage in total lunacy.

Las Vegas is a place where there is no such thing as a hotel, only a 'resort', and where there is no such thing as a 'resort' unless it is built around a core of five or six acres of gambling casinos.

Las Vegas is a place where every necessity and luxury of 'resort' life is either in the casino, or across the casino or through the casino, and where the only thing you can't find in the casino is the Exit.

Las Vegas is a place where free drink in ample proportions, dispensed by young ladies of ample proportions, is calculated to obscure the fact that there is something wrong with the mathematics of feeding a slot machine with about $5 worth of coins to collect a win of 50 cents.

Las Vegas is a place where a splendid $50 banquet in a gambling casino costs only $25 because well-fed clients gamble more readily than hungry ones. And even if the diners don't gamble, the dining-room incomes are adequately subsidised by the idiots who do.

Las Vegas is a place where the taxi queue of thousands of people per minute streaming out of the McCarran Airport is only about a yard in length because the city's cab drivers are as numerous and as diligent as a flock of black-backed gulls descending on an unattended Valentia fish box.

Las Vegas is a place where, when you ask the taxi driver what good stage shows are on in town, he tells you: 'The magic shows are best. You put money in the slot machine and press a button, and the machine goes "Ding Ding" and the money disappears. That's magic!'

I can second that! But one magical, value-for-money experience in Las Vegas was the *Mamma Mia!* stage show at the Mandalay Bay resort in 2005. It brought the house down. And for encore after encore, everyone who had access to an aisle – and many who had not – were up and dancing their hearts out.

Washington DC is splendid in spring when the cherry blossom is in bloom. We saw the opening buds in 1988, when, unencumbered and unimpeded by the 'security' extremes of today, it was possible to wander the city at will – the Washington Monument, the Air and Space Museum, and almost to the White House lawn of Ronald and Nancy Reagan. A memorable Washington dinner was enjoyed in the 'The Old Guard', 3rd US Infantry

Above the Hoover Dam, Nevada. Las Vegas is a veritable desert of red rocks and sand somehow made habitable by the engineering genius of this dam.

Headquarters in the company of Colonel Joe O'Connor – previously of the US Embassy in Dublin. Security considerations in such an Army HQ in today's atmosphere would surely bar this wandering Kerryman.

That other Washington monument, the 'Vietnam Wall', was a sobering sight in 1988. I gazed at it in sad silence, noting young people fingering the names of their fathers, old people caressing the names of their sons in that list of 58,000 who 'died for their country' in Vietnam. I wondered then about those who came home shattered in body and mind – to be rejected and forgotten. And I wonder now: when a memorial to the 4,000 Americans who 'died for their country' in Iraq is erected, shall it include a memorial to the uncounted, innocent, civilian victims of this trumped-up war about non-existent Weapons of Mass Destruction?

At least the overall losers in another Washington-inspired conflict – the American Indians – finally have their own monument. It is a monument to the one battle that they won decisively in the course of losing the overall war – the Battle of the Little Big Horn in Montana on 25 June 1876.

In November 2004, and again in 2014, I stood on that insignificant little

At the Crow Indian Reservation in eastern Montana, I stood at *The Spirit Warriors*, a brilliant evocative sculpture encompassing the concepts of earth, sky, wind and light, all dear to the heart of American Indian culture.

hill in the Crow Indian Reservation on the rolling plains of eastern Montana. I looked at the unimaginative granite obelisk that has occupied the Little Big Horn hillside since 1881 to commemorate the dead of Custer's 7th Cavalry. Then I walked one hundred metres to stand at *The Spirit Warriors*, a brilliant, evocative sculpture, encompassing the concepts of earth, sky, wind and light, all dear to the heart of American Indian culture.

Even though the fallen Sioux, Cheyanne and Arapaho had to wait 127 years, until 25 June 2003, for this Little Bighorn Memorial, its splendour – compared to the 7th Cavalry's granite pillar – tells me that Custer has been beaten again. And he is still under fire 130 years later. A bumper sticker seen recently on the back of a truck in Missoula, Montana proclaims succinctly: 'Custer had it coming!'

Our multiple visits to San Francisco did not exhaust all its offerings:

In October 2003, we were in San Francisco for the launch of the *Grace Quan*, a replica of a traditional Chinese shrimp-fishing junk.

25 October 2003 saw us enjoying a special San Francisco treat – on board the *Northern Light,* a 40ft Bermudan-rigged yawl, setting out from Redwood City with Valentia-born skipper/owner, John Cullen, and a motley crew of three of his friends, bound for China Camp State Park in San Pablo Bay, to attend the launching of a new vessel. This was the *Grace Quan* – a 43ft x 10ft replica of a traditional Chinese junk, newly built of local redwood and Douglas fir to the original design of the shrimp-fishing vessels that once worked San Francisco Bay extensively – between 1860 and 1910.

What with ceremonial dragons, drummers, fireworks and typical Chinese symbolism, it all led to an overnight sleepover on board the *Northern Light* – where we might have slept well but for one of our crewmen flushing the marine toilet in the middle of the night and illuminating the entire cabin with the glow of the phosphorescent sea-water pumped through the facility!

Some who were not familiar with phosphorescence may be forgiven for suggesting that the glow was caused by nuclear waste in the bay's waters.

Meanwhile, back in Valentia, the equivalent shipwright's trade was equally under weigh. A joy to note in 2003 was the work of Ciaran O'Regan and Declan Kirby, replacing planks in Dan McCrohan's 30ft *Christmas Eve*. Relatively easy to remove old planks frame-by-frame, perhaps, but the skill of shaping new planks into complicated curves to fit into an equally complicated jigsaw where there is not a straight line or a level base or a square corner was a joy to behold. Extreme tradesmen at both extremes of my compass! And in Valentia I did not dare mention the additional Chinese technique of skew-nailing the planks to one-another in the carvel design of the *Grace Quan*.

One other marine aspect of San Francisco became more and more tantalising year by year as I gazed seawards from clifftop vantage points at the

Repairs to Dan McCrohan's 30ft *Christmas Eve*.

Farallon Islands that appear on the Western horizon, or sink beneath it, according to the whims of the Californian climate. Some twenty-eight miles offshore, and seldom free from the ocean swell, the Farallons eluded me for twelve years, until a January day in 1999 when everything fell into place – good weather, calm sea and a convenient Oceanic Society whale-watching cruise out of San Francisco itself.

The Farallons – first designated a wildlife preserve by President Theodore Roosevelt in 1909 – have been strictly protected since 1969, and the restriction is now more appropriate than ever, as vested interests seek commercial access everywhere. Nobody, other than half-a-dozen seasonal resident biologists of the National Parks Service, may land there – a conservation policy that is certainly understandable to anyone with Skellig associations. Furthermore, with no boat-landing facility on the principal island, South Farallon – other than a 30ft derrick that can snatch an occasional National Parks employee from a dinghy – my craving was merely to get within

Sea lions basking in San Francisco. When seal-hunters arrived in the early 1800s, they wiped out all the sea lions from the Farallon Islands, which have been strictly protected since 1969.

100 metres' viewing distance of the overall magical place.

It is a magical place that was once almost devastated. When seal-hunters arrived in the early 1800s, they wiped out all the sea lions, northern fur seals and elephant seals for their skins and meat, and during San Francisco's population explosion of the 1849 Gold Rush, in an egg-hunting frenzy that saw two men killed in the violent, lucrative competition, the Farallons were stripped of seabirds' eggs to the extent that the guillemot (common murre) colony plummeted from some half a million birds to a few thousand. Not until the 1980s did the estimated numbers climb back to 70,000 and it was the late 1990s before they reached 170,000 again.

It being January, few birds were in evidence on our 1999 cruise; on the other hand, it being wintertime, grey whales were at the height of their migration through the area and, had we been lucky, we might also have seen blue whales, humpback whales, and great white sharks as well. But I did not care about such sideshows; I saw all 211 acres of the granite outcrops that constitute the Farallon Islands, studied every inch of them hungrily. And if I did see a grey whale or two – or ten – that was a bonus.

Only Americans could get enthusiastic about baseball. In October 2003, I managed to get a free ticket to a game between the San Francisco Giants and the Florida Marlins in San Francisco's waterfront ballpark.

The noise level was high. The Giants were being well-beaten, and – to the astonishment of my American contacts – I even quit long before the final whistle. Ultimately, the sportswriter in the *San Francisco Chronicle* would put the defeat more succinctly than any Irish sports journalist might write of a Kerry Gaelic football drubbing: 'The Bay area's baseball dreams are in a skid row pawnshop today, in a grimy glass case between a banjo and someone's mother's wedding ring.' He was so right!

By comparison, I recall the perfection of the San Francisco Symphony Orchestra, performing in its home – the Davies Hall on Van Ness Avenue.

Any Kerryman who has occupied a Terrace seat, looking down on the percussion section as Ravel's *Bolero* begins – Rat-a-tat-tatt, Rat-a-tat-tatt, Rat-a-tat-tatt – will never forget the splendid occasion. Equally memorable, on New Year's Eve 2000, Pat and I – together with Linda and her friend, Theresa Flanagan – enjoyed a side box on the main floor, while the music flowed and flowed. And – as if that was not enough, when the concert proper concluded at about 11pm, the stage was thrown open to all for dancing – dancing to this mighty orchestra as the midnight balloons cascaded down and souvenir 'San Francisco Symphony, 2000' champagne flutes were filled and refilled.

I still re-live the event every time I see the four souvenir 'San Francisco Symphony, 2000' flutes – not languishing in 'a skid row pawnshop in a grimy glass case, between a banjo and somebody's mother's wedding ring', but resting in a clean, bright, kitchen cupboard in Glanleam, Valentia Island.

There was another occasion on which I wished I could re-live my memories of the San Francisco Opera House's presentation of *La Bòheme,* but the Valentia Island Quarry/Grotto/cave at nine o'clock at night in August 2004 was not the place to do so. As an appendix to my education, this particular presentation of *Stabat Mater* by the Opera Theatre Company in this Valentia setting was probably quite valuable. As an entertainment, though, it was quite dreadful. But by knowledgeable folk, it was ultimately declared to be magnificent.

In truth, there was certainly much magnificence. The concept of putting on the show – any show – in a great hole in a Valentia mountain was magnificent; the gaunt, minimalistic stage set was magnificent; the harsh lighting, emphasising shape and shadow on the stark, dripping rock-face was magnificent, and the unrivalled acoustic quality of the cave was magnificent.

But, for me, the music was dismal. It may have been funeral music anyhow, but it was worse than that; it was funeral music for somebody who had no earthly chance of going to heaven! Dreary, dull, dreadful, with such long –

not even pregnant – pauses that I did not know it was over until someone began clapping – for whatever reason.

If the Opera Theatre Company had only presented *La Bòheme* in this quarry location on the Valentia mountainside at nine o'clock at night with a northerly gale whistling in from Dingle Bay, Mimi could have died much more readily than in the comparative comfort of a Parisian garret! As things were, *Stabat Mater* left me just as frozen as Mimi – 'tiny hand' and much more.

A final visit to Las Vegas in January 2011 would see me gambling seriously – not with dollars but with my 77-year-old life, zooming down a street-long, ten-floor-high zipline in the company of my then teenage grandsons Sam and Jackson Maloney! And a final visit to Butte, Montana would see me again at the local ski slope at Discovery Basin, wondering once more how any early Europeans crossed the USA's vast plains and impenetrable

In 1867, a trio of prospectors in south-west Montana knew enough about the new transatlantic telegraph cable to name their gold vein 'Atlantic Cable'.

mountains, and how a trio of prospectors here in the backwoods of the Rocky Mountains in south-west Montana, named their 1867 gold strike 'Atlantic Cable'.

Communications of any genre were not really at a premium 'out west'. The Pony Express from St Joseph, Missouri to San Francisco had only just begun its service in 1860 – as had the overland telegraph to the main west-coast centres of industry in 1861. The Rocky Mountain mining-city-to-be, Butte MT, was little more than a few disillusioned prospectors panning for gold in the Silver Bow Creek, and the neighbouring town-to-be, Anaconda, would not be founded until 1883. Nonetheless, on 15 June 1867, Alexander Aiken, John B. Pearson and Jonas Stough knew enough about the new (1865) transatlantic telegraph cable linking Valentia Island in Kerry with Heart's Content in Newfoundland to name their gold vein 'Atlantic Cable'.

The name 'Atlantic Cable' lives on today, not just as a commemorative roadside plaque to the long-dead mine near Anaconda, but also as the current name of a 'Black Diamond' ski run near the Discovery Basin ski resort.

In a recent skiing season, I found it secretly amusing that those expert skiers – extolling the virtues of the exhilarating 'Atlantic Cable' ski-run, and drinking their *après ski* hot chocolate in the related Discovery ski lodge – did not know that the old guy who had just limped in off the nearby 'bunny slope' was this Valentia man who had worked on the *real* Atlantic Cable for the final sixteen years and three days of its 100-year lifetime!

MY WINDOW

I f my *Béal Bocht's* wheelhouse, with its ever-changing views of my marine world, could be called a 'room with a view', so too can my Glanleam home be labelled. Whenever a day of Skellig cruising is completed, or when an evening stroll of local landmarks is done, or upon return home from a winter's sojourn in the USA, the northern half of my local marine world,

My Glanleam home provides me with a window on my marine world.

past and present, still lies in a panorama before my Glanleam windows to jog my memories of the waters and islands of Dingle Bay.

Twelve miles away is Inishvickillane, southernmost of the Blasket Islands, where God provided stones in perfect building-block dimensions for the oratory and monuments of the monks of early Christianity, for the home of the Ó Dálaigh family in the nineteenth and twentieth centuries, and for the mansion of one Charles Haughey in recent decades.

My *Béal Bocht* has taken me to Inishvickillane many times. Most of these visits were in the 1970s, ferrying groups of ornithologists involved in studies or surveys of the island's birds, notably some 6,394 pairs of storm petrels in the census of those times. It was in those days that I first heard from the ageing Ó Dálaighs that the island – still better known as 'Dálaigh's Island' – was soon to be sold to 'a Dublin man'.

View of the Blasket Islands from my front garden.

Landing facilities on Dálaigh's Island, even to this day, are basic in the extreme – a natural rock face for a possible 'step out' landing at a certain stage of the tide, or a tiny beach of shingle and boulders where a naomhóg or a dinghy might land on the rare occasion when the local Atlantic is calm and kindly.

In the 1970s, there was a conspicuous surprise for the newcomer on the beach of Dálaigh's Island – an aircraft's engine block lying amongst the boulders in the tidal zone and the propeller blades of the same aircraft in use as fence posts and handrails on the pathway scramble to the cliff top. These were the remains of the German flying boat, No. BV-138, of Coastal Flight, R. 906, out of Brest, that landed in the bay to carry out engine repairs, on 25 November 1940. It was finally abandoned on the beach by pilot Willi Krupp and his four-man crew, who lived on the uninhabited island for three days before paddling their way to the Great Blasket in their rubber dinghy and eventually being shipped by the Irish Navy's *Fort Rannoch* into army custody at Valentia – and ultimately to internment in the Curragh Camp for the duration of 'The Emergency'.

But there was a further Inishvickillane surprise for me, too, on a fine July day in 1972 when I noticed my young deckhand, Seánie Murphy, hammering some small, metallic object against a rock. In the shingle of the beach, he had discovered half a dozen shells from the aircraft's main armament, and he was trying to dislodge the projectile 'to see if the powder was dry'! Following words of advice in emphatic, understandable, deep-sea language, he desisted, and lived to sail another day – and follow the long road of becoming a seasoned seaman himself.

I had another visit to Dálaigh's Island a few years later – this time in the company of long-time friend, Lieutenant Commander Rory Costello of the Irish Naval Service. We were leaving Valentia on the *L.E. Deirdre* en route to a patrol of the Porcupine Bank west of the Aran Islands when we got a radio call from 'Tír na nÓg' – codename for the Haughey establishment on Inishvickillane – to come ashore and visit.

When the Chief calls, the Navy answers; we dropped anchor in Dálaigh's Sound and landed by dinghy on the beach where the engine block still stood out, clambered up the path where the propeller blades still doubled as fence posts, tramped our way past the old Ó Dálaigh home near Log na bhFhiolar, skirted the monks' ruined oratory, made ourselves comfortable in the sheepskin-draped, Micheál Mac Liammóir-designed dining-room furniture of Charles J. Haughey, gladly accepted numerous vodkas served in pint glasses, and enjoyed pleasurable – if fleeting – delusions of grandeur.

I had one more visit to Dálaigh's Island in that era. It was the summer of 1984, and this time was in a 25ft sailing yacht, the *Cailín Deas*. Pat and I were on a weekend sailing trip that was intended to include a circumnavigation of all the Blasket Islands, but in the approaches to Inishvickillane, a minke whale became much too interested in our progress, popping up on either side of the boat every few seconds. In a larger vessel, this might have

When the Chief calls, the Navy answers. The *L.E. Deirdre* heads to Inishvickillane.

Minke whale to port! A playful nudge from this beast could mean disaster for our little ship.

been an interesting experience, but this whale was easily the length of our boat, and easily twenty times our weight. Up, down, up, down, the whale's enthusiasm for a relationship continued – so close that every 'blow' shared its halitosis problem with us. The stench was quite dreadful, but the greater reality was the fact that a playful nudge from this beast could mean disaster for our little ship.

It was an experience remarkably similar to that of Muiris Ó Súilleabháin, described in 'The Whale' in *Fiche Blian ag Fás,* when he and his friends, Pádrig and Michael, and their sheepdogs were returning in their naomhóg to the Great Blasket island following a fishing trip near Inishvickillane:

We were in great danger – out in the middle of the Great Sound,
 a couple of miles from land and that savage, ravenous, long-toothed

monster up beside us, the way it had only to turn its head and swallow us up. I thought that at any moment we might be down in its belly. We were still pulling with all our strength, straining every sinew, the beast rolling alongside us, and from time to time giving us a side glance out of its two blue eyes.

Having no wish to continue such an intimate relationship in our small sailboat in the middle of the Blasket Sound, we promptly copied Ó Suilleabháin's flight, and set a course for the nearest land – Inishvickillane – and dropped anchor in the shallows off the beach. Our whale seemed reluctant to enter the shallow water, but we thought it safer to go ashore for a while and throw ourselves on the mercy of Mr Haughey's island realm, rather than submit to the attentions of the whale in its watery domain.

I still don't know which was the better choice. Pat – like young Muiris Ó Súilleabháin of old – managed to fall into a collapsed rabbit burrow on the island and hurt every bone in her body. Then, on our eventual departure, our anchor was fouled on the bottom – probably on another of Willi Krupp's three engines – involving much perspiration and perseverance to get under weigh.

Other whale-watching outings in more controlled conditions could not match the intimacy of that Inishvickillane experience. In January 1988, from Point Reyes lighthouse, north of San Francisco, we watched the Grey whales on their annual migrations between Alaska and Mexico. From Half Moon Bay, south of San Francisco, in 1990, I enjoyed a day cruise to see the Grey whales at closer range; on Maui, in the Hawaiian Islands, in January 1998, from the window of a condominium in The Whaler resort on Kaanapali Beach, we could watch the humpback whales cavorting close inshore, and on a whale-watching day-cruise out of the nearby port of La Haina, we found whales aplenty, but the outing was equally memorable for the fact that we had to remove our shoes and tread barefoot on the deck of this pristine cruise vessel.

Indeed, quite near to home, as a finale to a Puffin Island diving trip on 16 July 1997, we were lucky enough to have the company of a pod of five killer whales accompanying the *Béal Bocht* all the way from Puffin Island to Valentia's Bray Head. It is worth noting that since 2017, more and more whales – minke and humpback – have been noted and appreciated from cruise-boats within a few miles of Skellig Michael.

Pat and I never completed our *Cailín Deas* circumnavigation of the Blasket Islands on that 'minke whale day' in 1984. Nor did we get an opportunity to return to Inishvickillane in that era. Later visitors, however, even if they still had to contend with the island's hazards and pitfalls, had, at least, the use of a very fine, if politically questionable, facility: a large, yellow mooring buoy in Dálaigh's Sound.

Its presence was disclosed during the exposure of some interesting 'covert operations' in the area. In July 1990, word got out that the Navy, under the guise of 'Diving Exercises', and the Irish Lights tender, *Granuaile*, under the guise of 'checking the landing conditions at Inishtearaght', were involved in laying a private mooring buoy in Dálaigh's Sound for Charlie Haughey's motor yacht, *Celtic Mist*. Political flak began to fly; Dáil Questions were thrown and defended. But eventually, when the *Evening Herald* of 12 July 1990 pursued the story to its extremes, the splendid 'private' mooring was promptly re-classified as a 'public' amenity, and calm returned to Dálaigh's Sound, to the newspaper columns, and to the awkward political questions.

On 11 June 2005, for the first time in many years, I sailed my *Béal Bocht* through Dálaigh's Sound again on a lighthouse mission to Inishtearaght. No eagles soared over Inishvickillane's Log na bhFhiolar; the controversial mooring buoy – 'public' or 'private' – was no longer in evidence; the aircraft engine was no longer conspicuous on the pebble beach, and, symbolically perhaps, a recent landslide posed a threat to the zigzag pathway that leads aloft.

The neighbouring Inishnabro, 'Island of the Quern Stones', is also in my evening window's panorama, though distance and ocean haze mute the colour of its lush seasonal blanket of sea pink. Situated only a few hundred metres to the north of Inishvickillane, Inishnabro provides the northern arm of shelter for Dálaigh's Sound. It is an island well known in ornithological circles for its Manx shearwater colony of some 5,611 pairs. Lesser known are the island's dry-stone ruin and cliff-edge fort that, together, merit only sixteen, single-column lines in the *Archaeological Survey of the Dingle Peninsula*.

The landing on Inishnabro is as picturesque as it is difficult – a natural archway, scarcely three metres in width, leading to a tiny, boulder-strewn creek and a hazardous scramble from the rocky foreshore to the island's

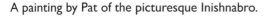

A painting by Pat of the picturesque Inishnabro.

colourful slopes. Bird-men are able for this; I have landed them there – and retrieved them – without any losses! But in matters of scenery, the most beautiful views of Inishnabro are not from the dry land, but from a boat near the eastern face of its northern cliffs where natural spires and arches, springing directly from the ocean, surpass the finest cathedral architecture in the world.

In my evening window's view, across the central saddle of Inishnabro, the peak of Inishtearaght peeps up. This is the most westerly of Ireland's islands. Its lighthouse is the most westerly station in the Irish Lighthouse Service; and Jim Lavelle could have died there on a summer's day in 1933.

It was lighthouse relief day. The lighthouse vessel, *Nabro*, had just landed him on the island for the normal six-week duty tour and motored off into the fog. It was then he took a heavy fall.

Having known Inishtearaght as it was in its busy, pre-automation days – its steep stairway access to the lighthouse yard and its difficult cargo-handling arrangements, including an aerial cable hoist and a winch-operated cargo trolley on an inclined rail track of perhaps 60 degrees – it is easy to see many opportunities for accidents.

During the construction of the lighthouse in 1870, Inishtearaght saw its first casualty when a workman was killed in a fall; in 1913, Assistant Keeper Morgan was likewise killed in a fall; in 1951, Keeper Eugene Gillan fell and tumbled a total of 95 metres – almost half the height of the island's peak – but survived; in 1973, Tom Joyce was awarded a gold medal for bravery in saving a colleague who was hurtling down towards a concrete pit; in 1974, a runaway 45-gallon barrel full of oil, tumbling down from the oil-store level, knocked Colin Myles-Hook over the edge of the loading platform 25 metres below, but he sustained only a grazed ankle.

If any such events occurred in our modern age, a rescue helicopter could be at Inishtearaght within the hour. But there was no helicopter on that

Relaxing on Inishtearaght, whose lighthouse dates from 1870.

day in 1933 when Jim Lavelle tumbled down. Radio communications did not yet exist, and in the fog, there was not even the option of recalling the *Nabro* with distress flares.

Fortunately, good neighbours were at hand. The Ó Dálaigh brothers of Inishvickillane – Tom and Paddy – were fishing in their naomhóg within hailing distance of Inishtearaght's south landing. They promptly took the injured Jim Lavelle on board, and they rowed him the nine miles to Dunquin – and to safety.

My *Béal Bocht* has made many Inishtearaght visits – landing bird-men for a week's ornithological work; landing seasonal sports-diving groups for their lunchtime break on the island's tiny dock and giving them the opportunity for a chat and an educational tour of the lighthouse with Principal Keeper, Paddy O'Shea; landing occasional items of lighthouse equipment; even landing coal there – eight tons of it!

Indeed, one such 'coaling' visit on a fine summer's day in 1972 could easily have been another Inishtearaght accident statistic. On the final lift of the day, the island's cable hoist gave way and sent five bags of coal crashing down on a platform only inches from where young Pádraig Kennelly and 'Mac' Browning had been loading the cargo trolley. They were neither

My *Béal Bocht* has made many Inishtearaght visits, including in 2013 with Irene Rogers.

injured nor hurt – but all were considerably chastened.

Beginish, smallest of the major Blasket islands, nearest to the Dunquin mainland, scarcely ten metres above sea level, and without any of the prominent features of its sister islands, appears or fades like a mirage before my Glanleam window according to the atmosphere of the moment. In the *Béal Bocht*, I have circumnavigated the island on many summer days, always mindful of the sunken reefs – too hazardous to contemplate – that lie in its environs. Luckily, most of my voyages have been optional, and generally en route to a mission or diving adventure.

But the intricacies of the tiny landing creek on Beginish's southern shore are well etched in my mind since landing there in the Valentia lifeboat's rowing cutter by the light of parachute flares in the black of a miserable, misty night on 2 February 1973, when Valentia lifeboat, *Rowland Watts,* was called to rescue two men who had been stranded on the island. It was a good and educational preview for a later visit on 16 June 1988, when I landed bird-men there on a splendid summer's day and finally availed of the opportunity to wander the island's 36 acres, viewing its precious colony of 170 pairs of arctic terns, and admiring the meticulous interior decoration of their nests – lined as they are with the blossoms of sea pink.

From my window, my eyes often linger on the island home of Peig Sayers, Tomás Ó Crohan and Muiris Ó Súilleabháin – the Great Blasket Island. The southern cliffs of its three-mile length occupy a goodly sector of my horizon, the steep cliffs and the *Quebra* shipwreck on its northern coast occupy a large sector of my diving memories, and the literary works of the island's scholars fill my reading hours with puzzlement.

With *Fiche Blian ag Fás* in one hand and *Twenty Years A-Growing* in the other, both open on Chapter 11, and with a chart of the Blasket Islands before me, I fail – in two languages – to make sense of the tale's directions for 'An Fiabhanc' or 'The Wild Bank'. An old copy of *Twenty Years A-Growing* indicates southeast; a new (2011) edition of *Fiche Blian ag Fás* says southwest! Others have already commented on this, and today's Poor Scholar and Poor Navigator may also conclude that it all refers to the location not of the Wild Bank, but of the Barrack Rock, about two-and-a-half miles south-east of Inishvickillane.

As I gaze out my evening window, pondering such harmless Blasket Island trivia, mental cameos of friends of other times – where decades mean nothing – appear before my eyes…

It is summer. The seasonal sun is sinking towards a golden horizon beyond those very Blasket Islands. Musketeer John Condon is on the phone.

'Hello, Des; we're in Valentia for a couple of days. Would you and Pat like to join Maggie and myself for a bit of dinner?'

It's an offer that cannot be refused. From an old quarry-worker's cottage on the slopes of Dohilla near Valentia's northern cliffs, we watch the sun complete its evening journey into the ocean. We eat well; we drink some wine; we sit around the turf fire, and we chat about old times, old cronies, old Musketeers, old boats, old adventures.

Pat and Marguerite cast their eyes to heaven as John and I pursue our usual interaction – 'speaking in parables' – having seemingly intelligent, technical conversations about nonsense! Total *ráméis*, all of it – but such fun…

But John cannot 'speak in parables' anymore.

My mental scene changes: The 'old' *Granuaile* is passing abreast of Cromwell Point lighthouse as she enters Valentia harbour. Her Captain, Musketeer Colin, will soon be coming to visit for chat and storytelling. Perhaps I can again try to persuade him to deliver his manuscript to a publisher – a splendid manuscript in text and illustration of all his days, nights and events in his maintenance circuit of every lighthouse and navigational buoy on the coast of Ireland.

But Colin cannot come to visit and chat anymore.

A new scene appears: It is July; World War II is over but there is still no petrol. It is Musketeer Adrian's birthday party on Beginish beach. We rowed over with his father, Freddy Mackey, in his clincher-built, olive-green punt, and we'll be able to sail home later on a gentle northerly breeze. A fire, made of beach-gathered driftwood, is already boiling a well-blackened kettle for the tea…

But Adrian cannot join a Beginish party anymore.

The *Crompton's* great anchor in Knightstown village.

'You're daydreaming again,' says Irene Rogers, knowing well that all my daydreams are good memories.

'Indeed,' I reply, and my reverie moves – not quite into today mode, but to distant summer days and to a friendship engendered when, in response to a tiny advert I placed in a British diving magazine, Irene and her husband, Ray Rogers, first came to Valentia in 1967. They came for a week's diving – and stayed for a fortnight! They came again in 1968 and came in 1969 – with baby Simon in a carry-cot – to visit us in Valentia and in Dingle during my stint on the movie, *Ryan's Daughter*. They came in 1970 and they participated in dives to recover the *Crompton's* great anchor that embellishes Knightstown village today.

Subsequently, Irene and Ray returned each year until 1975, when they moved to Hong Kong for some five years. But exchanges of postcards, photographs and Christmas greetings followed, year after year – even during their further adventures and travels throughout the Far East, Indonesia, India, Australia, New Zealand and Canada.

In 2007, Irene – then recently widowed – visited Valentia again, this time in the company of her son, Simon, and his fiancée, Silvana, and once more, old friendships were renewed and celebrated.

My windowsill reverie finally struggles up through the years. It is June 2010. Irene – in the course of a tour of the Aran Islands and the coasts of Clare and Kerry – comes again to Valentia. We stroll on Valentia's Bray Head; we paddle on Cahersiveen's White Strand. And while drinking coffee in Valentia's Skellig Experience Centre, she says, 'We must talk!'

This was a time when, following Pat's death in March of that year, I had already endured my fill of sympathetic talking and hugging. But this seemed different.

'Why don't you come down to my place at six o'clock and we'll chat over a meal?' I suggested.

She did. That was 27 June 2010.

In November of that year, Irene and I joined Céline and her Maloney family in Butte, Montana, for America's Thanksgiving festival; it was exactly that – a Festival of Thanks-giving by all for a new relationship of two senior citizens.

Likewise, New Year celebrations of January 2011 in Linda's San Francisco had an additional meaning for us – a *new* year, a *new* decade, a *new* beginning…

Add in our subsequent, annual winter visits to those cities and their hinterlands – dancing to country music in the Rocky Mountain fastness of Manhattan, MT; collecting my grandsons, Sam and Jackson Maloney, from school amid snow and ice in their Butte Central days; swimming in the outdoor, geyser-heated pool at Montana's Fairmont Hot Springs where the panorama of total snow and ice reaches to the poolside tiles; mastering the 'Muni' bus, street-cars and underground BART system in San Francisco's busy Bay Area. Visits to Irene's home in Wales and visits to her old friends in England have also become part of our new agenda. Likewise, a visit

Irene by Silver Bow Creek in Butte, Montana.

to Scotland to celebrate the wedding of Irene's son and daughter-in-law, Simon and Silvana.

Locally, in 2015, we repeated the boat trips of earlier *Béal Bocht* days – to Skelligs, to Puffin Island and to those Blasket Islands, now draped across our immediate horizon. Midsummer trips have been enjoyed locally. My new, 15ft punt, the *Béal Dúnta* – now boasting a 6hp outboard engine, a lug-sail, homemade from a 'misplaced' section of a *Star Wars* marquee, and with mast and spars homemade from recycled flotsam – took us to local haunts and beaches of yore. Exciting sailing days in *Steal Away*, our 15ft Wayfarer dinghy, passed many summer hours until its lively demands finally outstepped our athleticism and energy. There followed a brief flirtation with bicycles of appropriate vintage, but this too was soon terminated for similar reasons!

All these topics, and more, are the stuff of daily windowsill reveries and conversations – as is my happy decision to quit commercial boating in September 2014 and complete a timely sale of my *Béal Bocht* in 2016, undertaking then to write a completely new edition of my Skellig book – to be named *Skellig – Experience the Extraordinary* – which was published by the O'Brien Press, Dublin, on 28 March 2019.

And sometimes Irene and I even discuss my long-term dreams of writing a further book – a memoir, small or large, about old times, old events, and Old Musketeers. This is it!

APPENDIX:

A FISHY TALE

There were few topics more controversial on the coast of Ireland in the 1970s than the subject of drift netting for salmon at sea. Kerry was no different, and it is little wonder that we poked much fun where much fun was needed in those distant times – even taking to the stage! The show, *A Fishy Tale*, was performed in St Derarca's Hall, Valentia Island. Nobody remembers when – and participants are fading fast – but it had to be in 1978 or very shortly thereafter. It was a presentation of that time and for that time. And now it is history.

A Fishy Tale

Script: Des Lavelle

(Acknowledgement to Michael Egan for saving an original script until 2020.)

Setting

A local waterfront pier.

Props

A salmon net and netting needle and thread, a fish box, a lobster pot, a sack or two, a pocket-size whiskey flask, a shopping basket, a sheaf of notes, a salmon – real or artificial, a hand-held walkie-talkie, real or fake.

Special effects

A handful of feathers that will drop from overhead.

Offstage sound effects

Frenzied screaming of seagulls. Loud bang of a heavy gun.

Characters

Fishermen – Diarmy Walsh (D.), Brendie Murphy (B.), Pat Curtin (P.)

Garda Sergeant – Des Lavelle (S.)

Naval Captain – Michael Egan (Cap.)

No.1 Officer – John Quigley (No. 1)

Minister for Fisheries – Gene Sullivan (Min.)

Chairman of the Board of Conservators – Johnny Reidy (Ch.)

Singing group of girls – Ann Blincoe, Linda Lavelle, A. O'Neill, B. Blincoe

Dancer – Ann Blincoe

Musical accompaniment: Mary Gallagher

Opening chorus. (All on stage) Air of 'Fiddler's Green'.

Chorus (All): Wrap me up in my oilskins and blankets.
No more on the docks I'll be found.
Just tell me old shipmates I'm taking a trip, mates,
And I'll see them someday beyond Blasket Sound.

Girls: I walked by the dockside one evening so rare,
To see if the bailiff was anywhere there.
I heard an old fisherman singing this song:
My nets are illegal – too deep and too long.

Chorus (All): The Blaskets are islands or so I've heard tell,
Where fishermen go – if they don't go to hell.
Where the weather is fierce but the salmon do play,
And the bold Irish navy is not far away.

B. When the weather is fierce and there's even a gale,
The fish come aboard with a swish of the tail.
You pile them on deck – there is no more to do,
And there's thousands of pounds for the skipper and crew.

S.   They don't want a shark of a dogfish, not one!

But give them bradáns by the box or the ton!

And payments of taxes they'll nicely avoid,

As they're all on the dole – or they're all unemployed!

Exit all except B, left fixing a net that is hanging on the side. He is singing a bar of the same song.

B.   I heard an old fisherman singing this song,

My nets were illegal – too deep and too long.

Enter D. from right.

D.   You're fine and happy at your work, Brendie.

B.   Well, I'm making the best of it, although I don't know what the year will bring.

D.   What will it bring, man, but plenty of salmon, plenty money – like last year and the year before?

B.   Plenty bailiffs, I suppose, and plenty navy and plenty jail. I see tough times coming.

D.   You could be right. Didn't you hear about all that fortune of gear that was seized along the coast?

Enter P. from left.

D.   Hello, Pat. Did you see that thing in the papers about a quarter of a million pounds' worth of gear that was seized by the navy?

P.   Man, that's nothing! Isn't it well known that there's that much in Dingle alone – inside in every back yard? Salmon gear of every description … monofilament, 60 meshes-deep and the rest….Twenty miles of it or more … and there's three times that inside in Valentia … hidden in every bohaun … around turkeys and keeping in sheep!

B.   What's bothering me most of all is yer man the Taoiseach. He's out there on Inish-vickillane half the summer. And don't you know that half the Irish navy will be there watching – helicopters and corvettes and the-devil-knows-what.

D. (*recitation*):

There's a sleek and well-armed gunboat to the west of Dingle Bay,

Near the island where the Taoiseach settled down.

On board a busy bailiff who is watching night and day,

With gardaí who were brought in from out-of-town.

There were years of full-and-plenty when the fishing was supreme,

And the silver summer salmon paid the best.

But Decca sets and radars soon got rid of all the cream,

And the overdue repayments took the rest.

> The Board of Conservators told the bailiffs it must cease,
>
> And the poachers told the bailiffs it must not!
>
> And the gardaí in attendance had to try to keep the peace,
>
> With the navy torn in half between the lot.
>
> The benefactor buyers were the winners – very true.
>
> They made a princely profit from our work.
>
> And now they drive their E-types while the fisherman makes-do
>
> With a Volvo or a Peugeot or a Merc.
>
> There's a sleek and well-armed gunboat to the west of Dingle Bay
>
> Near the island where the Taoiseach sits on top.
>
> There's a broken-hearted poacher who is drinking night and day
>
> Since they told him that his caper had to stop.

D.   I'm going for a pint. 'Tis a dry kind of day.

B.   Leave one above for me; I'll be up soon.

Exit D. right.

P.   Do you think Charlie might ever take a bite of an illegal salmon himself, if he got it?

B.   Maybe our best chance is to take the first one we catch, land on the strand and send up for 'yer man' to come down…. Or take it up – personal-like – and deliver it into his hand?

P.   You'd never score there, poor man, there's Special Branch men as thick as gaosatháns hiding behind every rock. You'd need some sort of Fianna Fáil long-service medal to get beyond high water up.

B.   There's one hope that I see: since Charlie is such a great buddy with the Dingle crowd, maybe he'd call-off the pursuit a bit?

P.   Fat hope you have of that. Wasn't Charlie the first man to introduce the ban on monofilament when he was the Minister? He's hardly likely to go back on that now.

B.   Isn't that the very skill of the politician – to have the power to say 'yes' today and 'no' tomorrow, and make the people believe it twice?

P.   Power or no, there's plenty water between Inishvickillane and Valentia … and room for all.

B. *sings 'The Waters' (by Johnny Murphy, Valentia).*

> By the waters that flow round Valentia,
>
> There's one spot of fame and renown
>
> It catches the eye from the Quarry,
>
> As you gaze up the river to Town.

ISLAND BOY

And when we grew up into manhood,
And fishing got into our heads,
Out the lighthouse at six every evening,
And never a word about bed.

Our boat, she was one of the old ones.
She never saw any smart paint.
She was tarred from the keel to the gunwale,
And she carried the name of a saint.

We rowed her along nice and grámhar,
Till we came to the scoilt of Culloo.
We then took our oars off the water,
Deciding on what we should do.

We then steered a course to the North-West
Till we nearly lost sight of the land.
Bray Head far away in the distance,
Ceann Glas on the Coonanna strand.

We shot just an hour before darkness,
And then when we started to haul,
The first fish we hauled was a conger,
The most troublesome fish of them all.

The second we hauled was a halibut.
To us it appeared nothing strange.
For it was not our first time being lucky
To shoot on the halibut range.

We hauled away out in the darkness
With turbot and brill sure galore,
And the very next place you will find us
Is inside Johnny Pon's famous store.

Whenever we 'subbed', 'twas a fiver.

Whenever we 'subbed' sure at all,

For anything less than a fiver

To us would appear mighty small.

We always kept whiskey and cider

In bottles from E.J. O'Neill.

There was always a 'Céad Míle Fáilte'

At the Point from old Mother Neill.

But there's two of our crew gone to England

To toil night and day at the beet.

Sure nobody here would begrudge them.

We all know that sugar is sweet.

But now that the fishing is over,

And Spaniards are fishing too near,

I'll bid you 'adieu' for the present.

I'm off for a strange land next year.

P.   You'd better go for that pint or 'twill be gone flat.

B.   Come on up and we'll have two of 'em.

P.   No. No. I'm on the dry. I'll carry on here for a while…

B. exits right.

P. takes out a whiskey flask and has a slug.

*Enter **four girls** (left) to the offstage music of* HMS Pinafore.

1st girl: Where's Dad? Mum sent us down with some sandwiches and stores for the boat.

2nd girl: She said ye wouldn't be getting much in the way of food in Johnny Frank's.

P.   Dad was called away suddenly; he'll be back soon.

Girls *sing (modified)* HMS Pinafore *ditty.*

We sail the ocean blue,

And our saucy ship's a beauty;

We're sober men and true,

And attentive to our duty.

With the bullets free

O'er the bright blue sea,

We stand to our guns all day;

When at anchor we ride

On the Dingle tide,

We have plenty of time for play.

Ahoy! Ahoy!

The bullets free.

Ahoy! Ahoy!

O'er the bright blue sea,

We stand to our guns, to our guns all day.

We sail the ocean blue,

And our saucy ship's a beauty;

We're sober men and true,

And attentive to our duty.

Our saucy ship's a beauty,

We're attentive to our duty,

We're sober men and true,

We sail the ocean blue.

P. *takes charge of the basket of goodies.*

At the end of the song, the **girls** *exit (left).* **P.** *is about to follow them.*

P.   Fine young wans!

Enter **D.** *and* **B.** *(right) looking back behind them.*

B.   That new sergeant is coming down the pier.... We'll be caught for sure.

P.   Hide the gear – quick!

D.   Keep a cool head is our only chance. What could a sergeant from the County of Kildare know about fishing? We'll plan some pack of lies and he won't know the difference.

Enter **Garda Sergeant** *right.*

S.   Good day, men. 'Tis a fine day for the outdoor life.

B.   'Tis a poor day to make a living, sergeant. No copper – I beg your pardon, no penny – made for months now.

S.   Is that what you'd call a trawl net now, men – or what?

B.   'Tis a pollack net, sergeant – a very popular kind of fishing here in the summertime.

S.   There's good demand for them, I suppose, men?

P.   Great demand, sergeant; we export 'em at £6 a stone – and buy 'em back at £16 a pound as fish fingers.

S.   'Tis a wonder ye don't go after the salmon, men; there's a great money for them, they say.

B.   Oh, we couldn't do that, sergeant; we have no licences.

P.   You'd need to be a doctor or a teacher or maybe a parish priest to get a licence here.

D.   South Kerry gets nothing, sergeant. If we were in Kildare, we could get a licence over the phone from a TD.

S.   Isn't that the way? 'Tis always the law-abiding man that can't make a decent living. Of course, there's always the poaching…

B.   Oh, that's a low occupation, sergeant. You won't find anyone around here at that.

P.   In Portmagee you'll find 'em … not in Valentia. If we saw people at it here, we'd report them to yourself – to your good self.

S.   Well, good luck with the pollack fishing. I envy ye yer happy state in a grand place like this…

S. *sings: 'Valencia'.*

Valencia, in my dreams it always seems I hear you softly calling me.

Valencia, where the orange trees forever scent the breeze beside the sea.

Valencia, in my arms I hold your charms beneath the blossoms high above.

You loved me. In Valencia long ago we found our paradise of love.

In a magic dream of memory, I'll see you again,

In an old town far away beneath the skies of Spain.

O, city of tender romances, how shy were your glances,

And bright as the sunlight that glances through the orange grove.

(Repeat the first verse.)

S.   Well, I'll be off now, men, for a constitutional stroll. When are ye going to sea yerselves?

D.   If we had this job finished and boarded, we'd take off for Ballydavid and you won't see us here for a week. Good luck anyhow.

Exit **S.** *left.*

B.   What do you mean 'we won't be back'? Mustn't we be here on Tuesday to sign the dole form for that new fellow beyond?

P.   You simple garsún! Won't you do the same as you're doing all your life? Let your wife sign it and shove it under the barrack door Monday night. He'll damn soon get used to it – like all that came before him.

P.   *(Mimicking the sergeant)* 'Tis a wonder ye don't go at the salmon, men? Is that a trawl net, men? *(Shouts)* That's a monofilament salmon net, you clown! That net will kill plenty of stuff yet – in spite of yourself and your big blue suit!

P. *(looking offstage, left)*   God-Almighty-Father-Tonight – the navy is landed. Hide the gear! Hide the gear!

They cover the net with some sacks and exit fast, right.

Enter **Naval Captain** *and* **No. 1** *(left).*

Cap.   This is the place, No. 1. This is the hotbed of the salmon poaching. Right?

No. 1   Right, sir.

Cap.   You can hardly walk up this pier usually without falling over stacks of monofilament nets. Right?

No. 1   Right, sir.

Cap.   And it needs a good clean-up. Right … Right, No. 1?

No. 1   Right, sir.

Cap.   The local sergeant should have his preliminary instructions at this stage. Right?

No. 1   Right, sir.

Cap.   If we can just contact him now with a few final–

Enter **S.** *(left).*

Cap. *(continuing)*   Ah, sergeant, glad to find you. Right?

S.   Right, Captain.

Cap.   The minister is visiting the area today, right – to inspect the harbour facilities. Right, No 1?

No. 1   Right, sir.

Cap.   We must do the right thing, Sergeant. Right?

S.   Right, Captain.

Cap.   Orders are orders, Sergeant. Right?

S.   Right, Captain.

Cap.   We will communicate on Channel 72 VHF. Right? Now the poachers have better radios than us. Right? And they are monitoring our transmissions. Right? So, we shall need some sort of agreed code. Right?

S.   Gaeilge na telefíse, a Captaon. Ní thuigeann muintir Chíarraí in aon cor é.

Cap.   Ceart a Sheargaint? Ceart Uimhir a haon?

No. 1   Ceart a Captaon.

S.   Ceart a dhuine úasal.

Cap.   Synchronisí na húradóri. Ceart? *(Looking at watch)* A seacht a clog, díreach. Ceart, Uimhir a haon?

No. 1   Ceart a Captaon.

Cap.   Ceart a Sheargaint?

S.   Ceart a Captaon.

Cap. *(into walkie-talkie)*   Cliona, Cliona, this is Cliona 1. Right? We'll be back on board in ten minutes. Right? Prepare to get under weigh immediately. Right? This is Cliona 1. Out.... *(continues)* There's one other small matter, Sergeant. Right?

S.   Right, Captain

Exit **Cap.** *and* **S.** *(left), talking in whispers.*

No. 1 *sings 'The Last Farewell'.*

> There's a ship lies rigged and ready in the harbour.
> Tomorrow for old Dingle-land she sails.
> Far away from one land of endless sunshine,
> To my land full of rainy skies and gales.
> And I shall be on board that ship tomorrow,
> Though my heart is full of tears at this farewell,
> For you are beautiful – and I have loved you dearly,
> More dearly than the spoken word can tell.
>
> I hear that there's a wicked war a-blazing,
> And the taste of war I know so very well.
> Even now I see the foreign flag a-raising,
> Their guns on fire as we sail into hell.
> I have no fear of death; it brings no sorrow.
> But how bitter will be this last farewell,
> For you are beautiful, and I have loved you dearly,
> More dearly than the spoken word can tell.
>
> Though death and darkness gather all around me
> And my ship be torn apart upon the sea,
> I shall smell again the fragrance of these islands

On the heaving waves that brought me once to thee.

And should I return safe home again to Dingle,

I shall watch the ocean mist roll through the dell,

For you are beautiful, and I have loved you dearly,

More dearly than the spoken word can tell.

Enter **Cap.***, briefly, left.*

Cap. Right, No. 1. The launch is waiting, but they can wait more. Right?

No. 1 Right, sir.

*They step aside and salute as the Minister (***Min.***) and the Chairman of the Board of Conservators (***Ch.***) enter left.*

Cap. *and* **No. 1** *join the group.*

Ch. And over here, Minister, is the deep-water berth. It's only two feet deep because it was done by the coalition government – but is deep enough and big enough for the crowd that are here. There's none of 'em with big boats like Maguire or Joe Shea, so they don't need big berths....You'd hear them complaining about it once in a while, but they don't count for much. Most of 'em are voting Fine Gael anyhow.

And over here is where we put in the new water main for running water on the pier.... Indeed, I don't know what these fellows want it for; they don't wash – and God knows, they don't drink it.

Min. Of course, it will be a useful service for visiting yachts in the summer – the French and the British – people who appreciate such facilities.

People are entering, gaping at the Minister. Three **fishermen** *enter right.*

Singers *and* **dancers** *enter left.*

Ch. Oh, my goodness, we have quite a gathering here...

Minister *gets up on a fish-box to deliver a speech.*

Min. Ladies and gentlemen, I am happy to be here today in this little fishing village and to see all the fine fishing cruisers which indicate...

Ch. *(Interrupting in a whisper)* Trawlers, Minister, trawlers...

Min. ... the fine flock of trawlers which indicate a thriving industry. I would also like to mention that this morning in Cahersiveen I opened a private deep-water marina which can accommodate vessels with a length of 100 yards ... 100 feet, and a height of...

Ch. *(In a whisper, again)* Draught, Minister. Draught.

Min. *(Turning up his collar against the 'draught')* ... a height of 20 feet. It has the additional features that will wreck small punts and cheap vessels and get them out of the way. Now when I look around me and see all the herring bots piled high...

Ch.   *(Interrupting again)* Lobster pots, Minister. Lobster pots.

Min.   Lobster bots piled on the pier, it reminds me of my own home by the sea.... Well, by a river that flows into the sea ... the river Liffey at Kilcullen in County Kildare.... Now, we in government...

P.   *(Heckling)* What about salmon licences for the poor fishermen here?

D.   There are 360 salmon licences in Cork, and only nine in Kerry. What about that, Minister?

Min.   *(Continues, unruffled)* We in government are aware that there are many problems in the fishing industry...

B.   Well, that's a start. The last fellow said there were no problems.

Min.   There are massive problems of salmon poaching by unlicensed fishermen on the Kerry coast. And the new regional Board of Conservators, which will be sitting in Macroom...

P.   I hope they never get off their backsides in Macroom!

Min.   ... which will be sitting in Macroom, will get every help from me.

P.   Sit on a high stool and let yer legs hang!

Min.   The Board will have a fast new trawler to hunt down...

Ch.   *(Interrupting)* A fast cruiser, Minister ... a cruiser...

Min.   A new fast cruiser to hunt the poachers down on the high seas ... in gales of Force 2, or even Force 3. She will be equipped with a seagull outboard engine... *(He drops his notes,* **Ch.** *picks them up for him and gets them mixed up.)* ... and a forklift back-actor and a milking parlour... *(He sorts out his notes)* ... and driving this fine vessel...

Ch.   Skippering, Minister, skippering...

Min.   And skibbering this fine vessel will be a man well-qualified for the job, a man who has spent three days in the Glenans Sailing School in Baltimore and a full week in a seaside portacabin classroom by these very waters, studying under my good friend, the Chairman of the Board of Conservators, Mr John A Reidy, Esquire...

P.   My name is Patrick J. Curtin, Esquire, and what about a salmon licence for me?

Ch.   *(Mounts a fish-box.)* A Cháirde Gaedhil, Ask not what the Board of conservators can do for you. Ask what you can do for conservation.

D.   What about conserving the fishermen who are trying to scrape a living from the sea?

P.   Fatten the salmon for the Russians and the Icelanders and let Paddy go and scratch...

Ch.   Lady Spencer-Reidy and myself, joint owners of the famous Spencer-Reidy salmon weir, would be quite within our rights – granted by James the First – to claim every salmon that goes into that weir. But do we do this…?

P.   Ye do. And yer staff do it behind yer back and flog the salmon all over Munster.

Ch.   (*Unruffled*) We let our salmon free to spawn in the gravel beds and restock the whole river.

B.   There isn't a gravel bed left in the country by yerselves and yer Arterial Drainage…

Offstage sound effects of seagulls in the distance.

P.   What about the pig farms and the shi… all the slurry flowing into every river in the land? How can a salmon live in that? Yer all slurry anyhow. I'd like to knock yer faces sideways – like a pair of megrims… (*He attacks but is held by the sergeant.*)

Min.   Ladies and gentlemen. I would be happy to hear any opinions about these important topics…

LOUD CRIES of a flock of gulls offstage.

Minister is looking up and gets a splash of bird-poop (make-up) on his face.

Gull sounds continue, louder.

Capt.   (*On the walkie-talkie*) Cliona, Cliona, Cliona, we are under aerial bombardment … Mayday! Mayday! We need assistance… Mayday! Mayday! And send the launch at once. Mayday! Mayday!

Captain *is looking up and he gets the poop too… so does* **Garda Sergeant**.

Offstage, a loud bang, the feathers fall upon the scene and the gull sounds fade away.

Capt.   Here. Come on. We'll go to sea anyhow… Come on, lads.

        (*Addresses* **girls**) Take care of yerselves till we get back.

Exit right (hurried) **Minister, Chairman of the Board, Garda Sergeant, Captain** *and* **No 1**.

Exit **D.**, **P.** *and* **B.** *left.*

Dancer *dances 'Sailor's Hornpipe'.*

Singing group *performs 'Dingle Bay' (with some alterations).*

        The sun was sinking to the westward.

        The fleet was leaving Dingle shore.

        Their engines growling in the sunset,

        As they head for fishing grounds near Inish Mór.

        I also see a ship on the horizon.

        She is sailing to a country far away.

        On board are sailors feeling lonely,

        As they wave a fond farewell to Dingle Bay.

I see the green isle of Valentia.

I mind the caves around Lough Kay,

And gannets winging with abandon,

As they watch the silver shoals that come their way.

All through the night, men toil until the daybreak,

While at home their wives and sweethearts kneel and pray

That God may guide them and protect them,

And bring them safely home to Dingle Bay.

Offstage there is fierce commotion and shouting from the fishermen.

P.   Run … Quickly … Up here … Duck this way … Oh, God. I'm winded…

They rush on stage (left), **P.** *is carrying a salmon.*

They try to rush off stage (right) but are blocked by the sergeant who enters right.

S.   Stop! What's going on here?

Enter **Captain** *and* **No. 1** *(left) in pursuit of the three fishermen, and they are caught red-handed.*

Fishermen make pleas to **Captain**, **Sergeant** *and* **No. 1**.

B.   Honest to God, we weren't poaching at all…'Tis a salmon we took off a Spaniard…

D.   And we wouldn't do it again. Ever, ever…

P.   Oh, God, sergeant, I have a wife and kids – about seven kids … or more … and I have terrible hardship already… Be easy on us, sergeant…

Sergeant *sings 'The Bold Gendarmes'.*

We're public guardians bold yet wary,

But of ourselves we take good care.

To risk our precious lives we're chary.

When danger looms, we're never there.

But when we meet a helpless woman,

Or little boys that do no harm,

We run them in. We run them in. We run them in. We run them in.

We show them we're the Bold Gendarmes.

Sometimes our duty's extramural,

And little butterflies we chase.

We like to gambol in things rural –

ISLAND BOY

Commune with nature face to face.

Then to our beat when back returning,

Refreshed by Nature's holy charms,

We run them in…. etc.

At the commencement of the following verse, **P.** *comes forward and offers the salmon to the* **Sergeant,**

Captain *and* **No. 1.** *They accept. Handshakes all round. And it is clear that all is fixed.*

When gentlemen will make a riot,

And punch each other's heads by night,

We're quite disposed to keep it quiet,

Provided that they see us right.

But if they do not seem to heed us,

Or give to us our proper terms,

We run them in…. etc. *(All cast file on stage during these lines…)*

We run them in. We run them in. We run them in. We run them in.

We show them we're the Bold Gendarmes.

(Repeat.)

Curtain.